EMPIRE OF THE SEAS

EMPIRE
OF
THE SEAS
Thinking about Asia

SHIRAISHI Takashi

Japan Publishing Industry Foundation for Culture

Publisher's Note

This book follows the Hepburn system of romanization. Japanese personal names are written in conventional Japanese order: family name followed by given name. Except for place names found on international maps, long vowels in Japanese names and book titles are indicated by macrons. All personal titles and ages of the public figures mentioned in this book are as of the publication date of the Japanese edition in 2000. While some citations, references, and notes appear in the main text of the original Japanese edition, all of these have been compiled into the Notes and References section of this book.

Empire of the Seas: Thinking about Asia
Shiraishi Takashi. Translated by the Japan Institute of International Affairs (JIIA).

Published by
Japan Publishing Industry Foundation for Culture (JPIC)
2-2-30 Kanda-Jinbocho, Chiyoda-ku, Tokyo 101-0051, Japan

First English edition: March 2021

Originally published in 2000 under the Japanese title *Umi no teikoku: Ajia o dou kangaeruka* by CHUOKORON-SHINSHA, INC.

English publishing rights arranged with the author.

This publication is the result of a collaborative effort between the Japan Institute of International Affairs (JIIA) and Japan Publishing Industry Foundation for Culture (JPIC).

Jacket and cover design: Nishida Eiko, cooltiger ltd.

Printed in Japan
ISBN 978-4-86658-126-2
https://www.jpic.or.jp/

To the memory of
George Kahin and Uehara Takashi

Contents

Introduction

How should we think about Asia? What position has Japan occupied within Asia, and what sort of position should it occupy in the years to come?

This book represents an attempt to consider Asia and Japan's position within it in the context of a much longer, broader, span of time than the one we normally adopt. I regard Asia not as a stable structure made up of civilizations, topographies, and other elements, but as a regional system that comes and goes over the course of history. I look at how modern Asia came into being as this kind of regional system beginning in the early nineteenth century and transforming over the past 50 years, and how Japan has defined its position and navigated this system as it has evolved.

It goes without saying that to look back on history means to imagine our future. We can conceive of the future only as an extension of the past. The more intently we look at the present, the more our imagination becomes a prisoner to the now. Long-term visions are mistaken for idle dreaming, and short-sighted ideas confused with realism. But what seem like intractable situations today often reveal themselves to be more amenable to solutions a decade or two into the future. In considering the position that Japan should occupy in Asia, the most important thing is a sense of long-term strategic direction. The span of time we use to look back on the past and conceive the future is crucial.

History involves different categories of time, depending on the structures under discussion. Individual governments can be discussed in a framework covering just a few years, systems of government may have a history that spans decades, while states often have histories that stretch over centuries. The same can be said of regional systems and the underpinning structures of the geopolitical crust supporting them. After the end of World War II, the political and economic order in Asia was reorganized around the concept of a "free Asia," an "informal" hegemonic order led by the United States. Within this system, Japan has occupied a position as a semi-sovereign state, as the "workshop of Asia," and as "junior partner" to the United States. This order seems now to be undergoing major changes, following the formation of the East Asian economic sphere, the end of the Cold War, and the Asian financial crisis of the late 1990s. What changes are likely to occur in the regional systems of Asia? And how should Japan be involved? Posed this way, these questions imply a discussion of how we will conceive and build the future on a line extending from the history of the past 50 years.

But in thinking about Asia as a regional system, this is not the only span of time that exists. A regional system exists as a single structure, built on the foundations of the underlying geopolitical crust. During the nineteenth century, the tectonic plates of the region experienced major shifts. Leaving aside for now the question of what kind of regional order existed in East Asia in the eighteenth century, we can say with certainty that the Sinocentric East Asian regional order collapsed in the nineteenth century, together with the long-standing tribute system that had formed the foundations of that regional order. A new order, led by Britain from its interests in maritime Asia, took the place of this vanished system. Britain controlled points in Penang, Singapore, Hong Kong, Amoy, and Shanghai, and from a line connecting these points projected its power across maritime Asia and farther into mainland China through an "informal" British empire that extended far beyond its formal territories. The modern states and modern capitalist systems of East Asia came into being under this order, dominated and influenced by Britain's informal East Asian empire.

Britain also brought a new rationale for the order it created in Asia. Until then, regional orders and powers were things that simply existed. Britain created the concept of an idealized order that was juxtaposed with the reality on the ground and repeatedly tried to shape reality to bring it in line with this ideal.

This period saw the beginning of the grand liberal project. Ever since, regional orders have been formed within a relationship of tension between the real and the ideal. Although the nature and content of the project has changed, the liberal project is still with us today.

In this book, I propose to consider the birth, development, and changes in the East Asian regional system from the perspective of these shifts in the region's geopolitical tectonics. If political scientists think in terms of 50 years, and *longue durée* historians work on a scale that might cover 500 years or so, then I try to treat East Asian "modernity" as a single integral unit of time and consider the development of the East Asian regional order over the span of some 150 to 200 years, from the perspective of the various proposals for a regional order and the way in which that order eventually took shape.

How did this age begin? What ideas did people have of a regional order in East Asia in the nineteenth century, and what kind of order was eventually constructed? What changes did this bring?

Let us start our examination of these sketches for a regional system in Asia by looking at the case of Stamford Raffles, in Malacca, and his dream of a "new British empire."

Shiraishi Takashi
August 2000

CHAPTER ONE

Raffles' Dream

Malacca

Malacca (or Melaka, in the modern Malay spelling) is located on the west coast of the Malay Peninsula, around 150 kilometers southeast of Kuala Lumpur. Today, it's a two-hour drive down the North-South Expressway from the Malaysian capital, heading south directly after turning onto Federal Route 19. In the fifteenth century, Malacca was an important port on the east-west trade routes linking China with India and the Islamic world, flourishing as an important hub of the international trade in spices from the Moluccas (Maluku), the famed Spice Islands that were the site of violent sectarian conflict between Muslims and Christians when this book was written, and as an entrepôt for trade goods from Malaya and the nearby islands of Sumatra, Java, Borneo (Kalimantan), and Celebes (Sulawesi). At the time, Malacca was the capital of a sultanate that controlled the Straits of Malacca as well as the regions of Jambi and Palembang in southern Sumatra. Because of its strategic position, the city has been ruled throughout history by the dominant powers of the time. In 1511, Malacca was occupied by the Portuguese, who made the city the center of their efforts to establish an eastern trade monopoly and proselytize Christianity during the sixteenth century. From the middle of the seventeenth century to the end of the eighteenth, Malacca was under the control of the Dutch East India Company (*Vereenigde Oostindische Compagnie,* or VOC). In 1795, the British seized the city from the Dutch, and Malacca remained under British control until Malayan independence in 1957. Today, it is a popular tourist destination, home to a rich heritage of historical buildings left behind by its past as one of the chief cities of Malaysia.

Among the town's residents in 1811 was Thomas Stamford Raffles (1781–1826), the man who later gave his name to the Raffles Hotel and Raffles Place in Singapore. Historically, Raffles is best known as the "founder" of Singapore. But that founding did not take place until 1819. In 1811, Singapore was still a small fishing village of just a few hundred people.

At the time, Europe was in the throes of the Napoleonic Wars, and Holland was under French control. The Dutch maritime empire, which stretched from the Cape of Good Hope at the southern tip of Africa, through Ceylon and Java, all the way to the island of Dejima in Nagasaki, was largely dismantled in 1795 by the British, who, after the Dutch entered the war against Britain as an ally of the French, occupied the Cape Colony, Ceylon, and Malacca. In 1806, Napoleon had his brother Louis Bonaparte crowned as King of Holland, and in 1808, he dispatched the Dutch Jacobin Herman Willem Daendels to Batavia (modern Jakarta) as governor-general of the East Indies. This prompted a blockade of Java by the Royal Navy, and in 1810, following instructions from the Board of Control of the East India Company, the governor-general in Calcutta, Lord Minto, decided to occupy Java.

It was in the context of this plan to occupy Java that Raffles found himself in Malacca in 1811. Raffles had been born in Jamaica. In 1795, he joined the East India Company as a clerk at the age of 14, and arrived in Penang in 1805. He acquired a knowledge of Malay during the voyage

Malaysia and Malacca port, from a 1676 engraving, London-Greenwich, National Maritime Museum (Photo by De Agostini/Getty Images ca. 2003)

from London to Penang and once established there employed "natives" to help him compile a collection of sources documenting the customs of the Malay sultanates and their history. By the time he met Lord Minto in Calcutta in 1810, Raffles was already well known as an expert in Malay affairs. This was no doubt the main reason why Minto put Raffles in charge of drawing up a plan to occupy Java, as well as making him responsible for British strategy toward the "Malay kings" who ruled a succession of mostly small kingdoms stretching from Sumatra and Java, through Celebes (Sulawesi) to the Moluccas.

In Malacca, Raffles set up residence in the Bandar Hilir area, on the east bank of the Malacca River. To find the site today, stand with St. Paul's Hill on your left, then turn around and walk east past the Porta de Santiago gate, all that remains of the sixteenth-century Portuguese fort. An evocative account of Raffles during his time in Malacca has survived in the *Hikayat Abdullah*, a memoir written in Malay by Abdullah bin Abdul Kadir.

Abdullah recalls that Raffles hired large numbers of local people to collect books, specimens, and information of all kinds on his behalf. He hired a team of copyists, some of them working on old Malay stories and other texts, while others copied poetry. In addition to various kinds of Malay verse, Abdullah records that there were some 360 books in all, written in longhand: chronicles, histories, Malay documents on customs and law. Four or five copyists were employed to copy these and other materials that Raffles borrowed. Others were employed to collect samples of the local fauna and flora: plants and insects, centipedes, scorpions, mollusks, shells, coral, crustaceans, and wild animals. Abdullah was often asked to write letters to the various Malay kings: "Every day he ordered letters to be written for dispatch to the Malay States, the contents merely searching for a way to establish friendly relations between their rulers and the English and trying to gain their support. Every letter sent out was accompanied by presents and expressions of kind feelings." Raffles sent messengers to bring these letters to the Malay sultans and received presents and letters in return sending compliments and thanks.

Abdullah writes that Raffles "kept rigidly to his timetable of work, not mixing one thing with another." He wrote more or less every day. He had a large desk in his study, where he would spend long hours walking to and fro before lying on his back atop the desk, staring up at the ceiling or closing his eyes as though asleep. He would jump up suddenly to jot something down, then lie down again. At eleven or twelve o'clock he would go to bed. The following morning, he would walk up and down, reading over what he had been writing the night before. He would take three or four out of every ten pages and give them to a writer to copy out; the rest he would tear up and throw away.

Raffles and the Birth of the Second British Empire

Among the letters Raffles wrote during his time in Malacca was one dated June 10, 1811, to Lord Minto, the governor-general of India, in which Raffles outlined his plans for a "new empire." Minto was already in Malacca and was due to depart for Java within a few weeks. From Penang and Malacca, Britain now controlled the Straits of Malacca; the islands of the Moluccas were also under British control at the time. If Britain occupied Java, all the islands from the Bay of Bengal to the Straits of Malacca, from Sumatra, Java, Bali, and Celebes and the Moluccas, all the way to New Holland (Australia) would be brought under de facto British control. This was the perfect opportunity to dismantle the Dutch maritime empire and construct a new empire of the seas in its place. This was the main thrust of Raffles' letter to Lord Minto.

There was only one problem. The instructions from the Board of Control in London were to expel the Dutch from Java and then abandon the island. Minto objected to this idea and sought to place Java at least provisionally under British control. But whatever steps he took now, the long-term status of Java once the Napoleonic Wars came to an end was still uncertain. This was why Raffles' plan called for the construction not of a "formal" empire centered on Java but of an "informal

Bust of Stamford Raffles, ca. 1820 (Photo by Hulton Archive/Getty Images)

empire" that would establish a new regional order stretching across the maritime regions of the East Indies, from the Straits of Malacca to the islands of the Moluccas, with Britain at its head.

How did Raffles see this "new empire" in his letter to Lord Minto? His understanding of the geopolitical situation in the region was as follows. "The annexation of Java and the Eastern Isles" would bring the entire region from the Bay of Bengal to Australia under British influence. Apart from Java and several other Dutch possessions, these islands were made up of small nations that were "by no means fitted" to stand as independent states.

Of the "Malays," Raffles writes: "The tribes of which they are composed, though varying radically in customs, manners, religion, and language, and possessing very different degrees of civilization, have long been confounded by Europeans under the general appellation of Malays, a term which may still be retained for convenience. It may be safely affirmed, that about the period when the Europeans first began to frequent these countries, they were not only much more populous, but the governments were more strong and steady, and the inhabitants in general much further advanced in civilization. The Dutch, solely attentive to their own commercial interests, have, in their intercourse with these regions, invariably adhered to a more cold-blooded, illiberal, and ungenerous policy, than has ever been exhibited towards any country, unless we except the conduct of the European nations towards the slave-coast of Africa."

Having thus roundly criticized Dutch policy in the region, Raffles goes on to outline his proposals for "our Malay policy." It is worth reminding ourselves at this stage that the term "Malay" did not refer to a stable, well-established ethnic or political entity at this time. As Raffles himself admits in the passage quoted above, "the Malays" did not yet exist as a single group. The same is true of the various references to the "Chinese" and the "Arabs" in the passages that followed. But this was to change: British policy was designed and put into practice on the basis of these imprecise categories. Over time, this policy transformed these nebulous groups from vague theoretical concepts into existing categories in society. I will have more to say about this later. For now, I propose to consider Raffles' proposals for "our Malay policy."

Raffles' vision of a "new empire" (map shows modern state boundaries and place names)

Broadly speaking, the policy consisted of two pillars. The first was to use traditional sources of authority to establish the foundations of British suzerainty in the region. According to Raffles, the Malay kings known variously as "sultans" and "rajas" held significant authority within their own kingdoms—but in previous times, they had formerly acknowledged the suzerainty of "the King of the ancient and powerful state of Majopahit on the island of Java . . . who had the title of '*bitara*.'" The authority and prestige of today's Malay kings, he suggested, could be similarly enhanced if they placed themselves under the protection of a similar great king, or maharaja. If this were the case, they were not likely to oppose the idea. If they could be persuaded to grant the title of "*bitara*" to the governor-general of India, Britain would achieve "a general right of superintendence over, and interference with, all the Malay states." In other words, suzerainty. This was the first pillar of Raffles' proposal for "our Malay policy."

The second element was the idea that Britain should establish a "chain of posts" in the islands of the East Indies and use the links connecting them to project British power. Raffles focused particularly on the islands of Bangka, Bali, Celebes, and Jelolo (Halmahera). Each of these islands held a strategic position within the surrounding seas. And all of them had resisted Dutch control. By forming alliances with the powerful kingdoms in these islands, Britain would make them responsible for maintaining order in the islands and stimulating regional trade. This was the second pillar of Raffles' proposal.

Raffles particularly emphasized the role of the Bugis (Buginese) and Macassarese peoples who inhabit the region around the port of Macassar/ Makassar (also known as Ujung Pandang) in the south of Celebes (Sulawesi). The Bugis live on the southwestern peninsula of the island and have many points of similarity in language and culture with the Macassarese who inhabit the southernmost part of the peninsula; the two groups are often referred to together as "Bugis-Macassarese." For centuries, these ethnic groups were known throughout maritime Southeast Asia as pirates, mercenaries, and traders. During the seventeenth and eighteenth centuries in particular, they were active across a vast region, stretching from Johore and Selangor in the south of the Malay Peninsula to New Guinea and the northern coast of Australia. Regarding the "Bugis and Macassar tribes," Raffles notes that "the Hollanders" have fomented civil wars and carried out a ruthless slave trade, and that the local people have become fragmented and weakened as a result. The British should therefore adopt a policy that is "exactly the opposite of this," he writes. British policy should be to protect the Bugis and Macassarese, and thus "create a powerful and active nation in [Celebes] the centre of the eastern islands," which would share the benefits of an alliance with the British.

The Bugis and Macassarese, then, were to be the main allies of the British in this new empire. Who would be their main rivals?

First of all, Raffles warns against the Chinese. In their colonies, he explains, the Dutch policy was to oppress the Malays and Javanese "natives" and support the Chinese. But the Chinese are not "children of the soil," and tend to follow the practice of "remitting the fruits of their industry to China." He describes the Chinese as "supple, venal, and crafty," and writes that for that reason they recommended themselves to the equally "crafty, venal, and speculating Hollanders." Since the arrival of the latter, they have made themselves the "agents of the Dutch" and have acquired a virtual monopoly on revenue farming and government contracts. There is hardly an influential Dutchman in the colonies, he writes, who is not dependent on the Chinese in his "contracts and speculations." But the Chinese are merely "temporary residents" in Java; their only objective is to make money. And although the "improvement of the people" has never been a priority with the Dutch in their rule, there are aspects of the Chinese way of doing things that have "not failed to open the eyes of the Dutch themselves" to the nature of the people they are dealing with. A recent report by "the counsellors of Batavia," he writes, refers to the Chinese as a "pest." When the Chinese acquire agricultural land, the rent for rice paddies jumps to five times its previous level. Wherever they have formed extensive settlement, he writes, the native Javanese have no choice but to abandon the district or become slaves of the soil. The situation is similar outside Java. Throughout the Malay kingdoms, the Chinese control the port duties and seek to monopolize trade. And "from their peculiar language and manners," they "form a kind of separate society in every place where they settle," which gives them an advantage over their competitors in arranging monopolies of trade. It is therefore vital to guard against the Chinese, he writes, both commercially and politically.

Raffles also warns against the Arabs and the Americans. The Arabs, he writes, have tried like the Chinese to monopolize trade ever since they first visited the Malay kingdoms. But they are even worse than the Chinese. The Chinese, at least, are "industrious," but the Arabs do not work: they are "useless and idle consumers of the produce of the ground." And these are not rich Arabian merchants with large reserves of capital: "the Arabs who frequent the Malay countries . . . prey on the simple, unsuspicious natives," moving from port to port and claiming the titles of "*sheik*" (elder) and "*sayyid*" (a descendant of the Prophet), worming their way into the favor of the Malay chiefs and procuring the highest offices of the states, which they "hold like robbers."

For example, the "old Sultan of Pontiana" (Pontianak, in western Borneo) took steps to prevent the Chinese from farming his port duties or monopolizing his trade. But even he was "duped" by "Arab adventurers." The present sultan is not so easily deceived, but Arab traders who arrive direct from Arabia are still allowed to trade duty free. But no one, Raffles writes, should be given special exemptions from duty, just because they happen to hail from "Muscat, Mocha, or Jidda." These cases illustrate "the necessity of our establishing an equal and uniform system of port regulations through the whole of the Malay countries."

The problem posed by the Americans was of a different nature from that presented by the Chinese and Arabs. They had started to arrive in the region around the time of the embargo of Java and to frequent the Moluccas "for the purpose of picking up articles for the Chinese market." They had lately begun to widen their sphere of operations. If Americans, who are "certainly not particularly well affected to the English" (not long after their independence from Britain), and who are "such active and enterprising traders," are allowed to trade on equal terms with ourselves (i.e., the English), Raffles writes, "it will inevitably be injurious to our commercial interests."

The only purpose of the Americans "wherever they go" is "commercial adventure." And there was a high demand for firearms, which would be considered the most profitable articles. Left to their own devices, the Americans would no doubt soon be selling firearms everywhere throughout the eastern islands.

Looked at in these terms, "our policy" was clear. The policy of the Dutch was to monopolize trade and control production. They could not understand that "in the long-run it must be more profitable to make smaller profits on a larger capital than larger profits on a smaller capital." Our policy, by contrast, must be to encourage free trade. In this sense, "our policy" would be quite different from what had preceded it. But there were some aspects that were worth retaining from the Dutch.

The Dutch had worked to drive all rival forces from the East Indies, both native and European, except in certain ports that were under their control. The Dutch had done this to ensure themselves a trade monopoly. But the same policy could also be used to encourage free trade. Trade would be allowed only in certain designated ports within each region of the seas and forbidden in all other surrounding ports. This would make it possible to support certain kingdoms as allies and make them responsible for maintaining order in the surrounding seas. Combining political and trade policy in this way would make it possible to maintain law and order in the maritime areas around these powerful ports and stimulate regional trade. This in turn would have the effect of promoting "the civilization and general improvement of all the Eastern nations." The "policy of establishing certain determinate and regular ports as emporiums of trade" would prevent the islands and the trade among them from being overrun by "unprincipled adventurers, chiefly Chinese, Arabian, and American." It would strengthen the "interest of the British nation" and ameliorate the condition of the natives in the Malay nations. This, then, should be the purpose of "our policy."

These arguments formed the pillars of Raffles' policy for constructing a new type of empire. As we have seen, Raffles envisaged a maritime empire based on free trade—its purpose was not controlling territory or land. The empire would be built on the foundations of British military power. By annexing Java, the British would drive Dutch and French forces from the region's seas and establish British military superiority across a maritime region extending "nearly from the Bay of Bengal to our settlements on the continent of New Holland." The British would then cultivate trading bases in the chief ports of the powerful kingdoms between the Straits of Malacca and the Moluccas. The prosperity brought by this trade would enhance the power of the kingdoms, and the maintenance of the new regional order would also be in the interests of these kingdoms. The Malay kings (rajas) would be encouraged to look to the director-general of India as a maharaja, and in the name of this maharaja, Britain would introduce to these Malay countries "equal and uniform" laws, systems, government, and policies—what we might describe today as "global standards." In this way, the British would build a liberal political and economic order in the East

Indies. In this sense, Raffles' policy ideas represented a proposal for a kind of new regional order as the Pax Britannica became a reality in Southeast Asia and for one of the first major liberal projects to incorporate the spirit of Adam Smith.

The Contradictions of the Early British Order

In fact, however, the order that took shape in Southeast Asia between the 1820s and the 1860s was something quite different from Raffles' picture of Britain's "new empire." Firstly, Britain projected its power not from a line that stretched from the Bay of Bengal through the Straits of Malacca, Bangka, Bali, Celebes, and Halmahera to "our settlements on the continent of New Holland," as Raffles had predicted, but along another line that reached from Calcutta to Hong Kong and Shanghai, via Penang and Singapore. This meant that Britain's "new empire" was constructed not in the East Indies but in East Asia. Secondly, this gave rise to a British-dominated free trade empire in Southeast Asia with its center at Singapore, "founded" by Raffles in 1819 and incorporated as part of the Straits Settlements colony together with Penang and Malacca in 1826. From these bases, Britain controlled the Straits of Malacca and extended its influence across the Malay Peninsula, the east coast of Sumatra, the Riau Archipelago, and Borneo. But Britain's chief allies in building and maintaining this free trade empire turned out to be the Chinese, the very people Raffles had warned against. In time, Singapore grew to become a major center of overseas Chinese in Southeast Asia.

Why did things happen this way? In terms of international politics, the answer is quite simple. In Europe, the Napoleonic Wars came to an end with the signing of the Treaty of Paris between France and the anti-French Allies. According to the terms of the peace settlement, Britain gained control over Malta, the Cape of Good Hope, and Ceylon, while Java was handed back to Holland in 1816. The British invasion of Java in 1811 had prompted thoughts of building a "new empire" that would reach from the Straits of Malacca to the Moluccas; the return of Java to Dutch control now caused Britain to lose interest in the East Indies. Further impetus was given to this shift of interests by the fact that opium became the biggest article of export in China trade around this time. At the time, Europeans known as "country traders" received permission from the East India Company to trade in maritime East Asia. Now that opium had become the main article of trade with China, these traders no longer needed to rely on the East Indies for commodities to trade with China. After the Opium Wars, new centers of British interest were established along the Chinese coast following the ceding of Hong Kong and the establishment of the "treaty ports." An "informal" British empire grew up around a line that connected Penang and Singapore with Hong Kong and Shanghai.

The term "informal empire" conveniently captures the nature of the British-led regional order established in East Asia and Southeast Asia between the 1820s and the 1860s. The concept refers to the wider sphere of British influence, as opposed to the colonies, dominions, concessions, and treaty ports that made up the formal empire. One sphere of influence grew up around the Straits Settlements in Southeast Asia. Another sphere of influence centered on Hong Kong and Shanghai. Together, these spheres constituted an informal British empire that stretched across much of East and Southeast Asia.

But this alone tells us nothing about why it was the Chinese who became Britain's main allies in this Singapore-based free trade empire and nothing about what this meant. Before we go any further, I should add a note about the Bugis and Macassarese, who Raffles imagined would become Britain's chief allies in its "new empire" in 1811. I do not mean to suggest that these groups did not also help to support Britain's free trade empire in Southeast Asia. Bugis trading ships made their way to the Straits of Malacca on the southwest monsoon from July to October every year, sailing from their bases in Macassar in southern Celebes, Banjarmasin in southern Borneo, Bali, and Sumbawa (east of Bali). By the end of the eighteenth century, these traders wielded significant influence and power over the Riau Archipelago to the south of Singapore. Following the establishment of a British settlement in Singapore, these Bugis traders began to arrive in Singapore as well. By the 1830s, the entirety of the trade between Singapore and Celebes, and 90 percent of the trade between Singapore and Borneo, was apparently in the hands of the Bugis and Macassarese.

There were two trading seasons in Singapore at the time. The first, roughly from December to February, was known as "junk season," when Chinese junks arrived on the northeast monsoon from ports in China and Siam (Thailand). The second was the "Bugis season." By the 1830s, more than 200 sailing vessels, each carrying around 30 Bugis and Macassarese traders, would arrive in Singapore on the southwest monsoon between July and October before returning to Borneo and Celebes when the northeast monsoon began in November. But this "Bugis season" peaked in the 1830s and gradually lost importance in the decades that followed. The Bugis declined rapidly as a proportion of the total population of Singapore, from 18 percent in 1824 to just 1 percent in 1850. Raffles' expectation that the Bugis would become Britain's chief allies in their new endeavor became further divorced from reality as time passed.

So why did the Chinese become Britain's allies, and what significance did this have? First, let us confirm two points of fact. The first of these is population. In 1824, the population of Singapore was 11,000. This grew to 52,000 in 1845, and to 80,000 by 1850. These numbers may not seem particularly impressive: they might represent a medium-sized provincial town today. But in the early nineteenth century, the whole of Malaya had a population of less than 1 million, and Batavia (Jakarta), one of the biggest cities in Southeast Asia, had a population of around 150,000. In this context, the growth of Singapore was quite remarkable.

As time passed, Singapore became more and more a Chinese town. To see the truth of this, it is enough to look at the proportion of the total population made up by Chinese over time. In 1824, the Chinese represented 31 percent of the population; by 1850, they made up 62 percent. At the same time, the sex ratio of the Chinese population was quite uneven. In 1830, there were 11.3 Chinese men for every Chinese woman in Singapore. In 1860, men outnumbered women by 14.4 to 1, and by 5.1 to 1 in 1881. In simple terms, nineteenth-century Singapore developed as a kind of giant bunkhouse for Chinese laborers and traders.

Another important thing to note is trade and public finance. In 1825, the total value of Singapore's trade was 2.6 million pounds. By 1859, this figure had increased fortyfold, to more than 100 million pounds. This

A view of Singapore with American, French, and British ships, ca.1850 (oil on canvas) (Photo © Christie's Images / Bridgeman Images)

was equivalent to two-thirds of the total trade of the Dutch East India Company (VOC) in the same year. At the same time, more than two-thirds of the revenue of the Straits Settlements government came from farming out the right to sell opium and other items. Revenue from the opium farms alone represented fully half of the total government income. This remained more or less constant throughout the nineteenth century. Given this, it is fair to say that although Singapore did develop as the center of a British free trade empire in Southeast Asia, as Raffles had envisaged, the expenses of building and maintaining this free trade empire were defrayed by farming out monopoly rights, particularly those relating to the sale of opium, that is, "drug money."

How did this happen? The answer is simple. Singapore developed as a free port. The growth of Singapore's trade shows the success of this model. But in a free port, there is no income from duties. The state apparatus in the Straits Settlements at the time was still small, a kind of baby leviathan still taking its first toddling steps. When responsibility for the Straits

Settlements was transferred from the English East India Company to the direct control of the Colonial Office in London in the second half of the 1860s, for example, the total staff comprised fewer than 300 people, including soldiers. Even so, this small state still needed money. The question was: How to raise the necessary funds?

From its founding, two economies developed in Singapore. One was the free port trade. The central players in this economy were the British "country traders" and the Chinese intermediaries who won their trust, mostly from Malacca. The overwhelming majority of the Chinese in Singapore in the mid-nineteenth century had not come with the intention of settling permanently. The fact that men outnumbered women by 11.3 to 1 in 1830 shows this fact quite clearly. The British country traders preferred not to deal with these new arrivals. The risk was simply too great: you might hand over a delivery of merchandise one day, only to find that the merchant was no longer there when you went to collect payment. By contrast, the Malacca-born Chinese had in most cases been resident in Malaya for several generations. They had wives and families there, used Malay in their daily lives, and often spoke a smattering of English as well. From the perspective of the British traders, these "respectable Chinese" were trustworthy partners: people you could do business with.

The other economy that grew up in Singapore involved the cultivation of pepper and gambier, a tannin-heavy product obtained from the leaves of a vine and used for tanning leather, as a dye, and in medicines. In the nineteenth century, the leaves were boiled and allowed to harden, and the resulting substance used instead of pitch to caulk boats. Chinese people had been cultivating pepper and gambier in Singapore since before Raffles' arrival. Chinese plantation owners borrowed money from Malacca-born Chinese and used coolie labor to open plantations in the interior of Singapore, where they grew pepper and gambier for the Chinese market. This economy expanded massively after the "founding" of Singapore. The plantations gradually spread farther inland along rivers, and by the 1820s pepper and gambier were being cultivated along what is now Orchard Road. By around the 1840s, these plantations were expanding farther afield, spreading from Singapore to neighboring Johore in the south of the

Malay Peninsula, as well as south to the islands of the Riau Archipelago, in what is now part of Indonesia.

There were only two ways for the Straits Settlements government to raise funds: either from trade or from the pepper and gambier plantations. While the Straits Settlements remained free trade ports, the government could not raise money from levying of duties. The only option left was to earn revenue from the cash crop economy that had grown up around the cultivation of pepper and gambier. The problem was that this entire economy—capital, labor, and markets—was under the control of Chinese "secret societies" such as the triads and the Ghee Hin Society. All the Chinese—from the "respectable" Chinese of Malacca to the plantation owners and the coolie laborers—were affiliated with these syndicates. Traders arrived in Singapore via this network, used coolie labor provided and organized by the secret societies to cultivate pepper and gambier for the Chinese market, and used this same network to send their money home again. This is one reason that opium farming and other such revenue farming activities were so crucial. Following a purely formulaic tendering process, in exchange for a certain amount of money the British farmed out the monopoly rights over opium sales and collection of taxes on gambling to the "respectable" Chinese from Malacca who had won their trust. The secret societies acted as subcontractors for the "respectable" Chinese, offering opium and gambling to the coolies who worked on the plantations. In this way, an alliance was formed between the Straits Settlements government and the respectable Malacca-born Chinese and the secret societies. The toddling leviathan grew fat by siphoning off money from the overseas Chinese network.

When we look at the situation in this way, it becomes clear that two opposing principles were in operation in the British free trade empire that took shape in nineteenth-century Southeast Asia. On the surface was the principle of free trade, as represented by the Straits Settlements government, the British country traders, and the "respectable Chinese." The other involved the network of the overseas Chinese, controlled during the nineteenth century by the Malacca-born "respectable Chinese" and the secret societies. This network reached from the Straits Settlements to the Malay Peninsula and the Riau Archipelago. Throughout the area of its influence, free trade was the principle followed on the surface, while revenue from opium farming (that is, the monopolies thereof) covered the expenses of the state. This system continued for as long as the British had no choice but to accept the secret societies as a necessary evil. But tension always existed between the two principles. From the perspective of liberalism, the overseas Chinese network was a mess of opaque personal relationships and unacceptable monopolies. When territorial squabbles among the secret societies led to public disturbances in the Straits Settlements and the tin mining areas of the Malay Peninsula, this lack of transparency suddenly became a major problem for the authorities, marking the beginning of the next generation of the liberal project. In the late nineteenth and early twentieth centuries, the "civilizing mission" replaced free trade as the preoccupation of empire and was spoken of as the "white man's burden."

CHAPTER TWO

The Bugis Sea

In his 1811 letter to Lord Minto on the eve of the British invasion of Java in that year, Raffles had proposed a "new empire" stretching from the Straits of Malacca through Bangka, Bali, and Celebes, all the way to New Holland (Australia). The proposal envisaged that the British would construct this new empire on the back of an alliance with the Bugis people. By the middle of the nineteenth century, a British free trade empire had indeed grown up with its center at Singapore, but it was something quite different from the "new empire" that Raffles had imagined. Firstly, the empire was built in the maritime region stretching from Penang and Singapore to Hong Kong and Shanghai—not, in other words, in the East Indies but in East Asia (as defined in the World Bank's report on the "East Asian miracle"). In more general terms, the new empire encompassed the maritime region between Southeast Asia and East Asia. Secondly, Britain's main allies in constructing this empire were not the Bugis but the Chinese, who Raffles imagined would be the enemies of a new British empire in the region. Singapore developed as a major center of the Chinese network

Etching of Singapore by Raffles titled, "View of Singapore Town & Harbour taken from the Government Hill," possibly after Augustus Earle, published in *Memoir of the Life and Public Services of Sir Thomas Stamford Raffles* by Lady Sophia Raffles, 1830 (Courtesy of the National Museum of Singapore, National Heritage Board)

in Southeast Asia, and the Chinese network was intimately linked to the British free trade empire from its inception.

The challenge is how to explain this. I have already discussed why the British free trade empire grew up not in the East Indies but in East Asia. In summary: Java was returned to Dutch control following the end of the Napoleonic Wars. This meant that the British government soon lost interest in the East Indies. Around the same time, opium became the most important article of export in the China trade. British country traders no longer needed to rely on the East Indies for articles to trade to China, and following the Opium Wars, the ceding of Hong Kong to Britain and the establishment of treaty ports saw Britain establish bases along the Chinese coast. In this way, the British free trade empire grew up in the maritime region stretching from Southeast Asia to China. But this does not explain *why* Singapore developed as a center of the Chinese network in Southeast Asia or *why* the overseas Chinese network was so closely linked from the outset to the British free trade empire.

Merely stating the facts in this way does not constitute an explanation for why things happened the way they did. We have seen that the British free trade empire was established in the maritime region between Southeast Asia and China rather than in the East Indies and that Singapore developed as a center of the Chinese network. And we have seen how the contradictory principles of free trade and the Chinese network operated at the

same time within this new empire. But these facts alone do not constitute an explanation. A look at the trade statistics confirms that Singapore developed as a center of trade in Southeast Asia from its founding, and that the trade with China accounted for a mere 15 percent or so of Singapore's total trade throughout the nineteenth century.

Another explanation, perhaps more intellectually appealing, looks at the tributary trade system that previously existed in the region as a distinctly Asian type of international order. During the nineteenth century, this was incorporated into the modern international system following the arrival of the Western powers and the establishment of the British free trade empire. What kind of regional order existed in Asia prior to the coming of the Western powers? In his analysis of the early Asian order, Hamashita Takeshi has argued that Asia in this period is best considered not as a land-based but a sea-based world made up of a number of interconnected maritime areas. According to this view, China was able over the course of history to expand its Sinocentric order steadily outward toward the periphery of this maritime Asian world. Essentially, China was able to transform the attractiveness of its markets into political and cultural power through the tributary trade system. During the Ming and Qing eras, in which China's prominence as an empire made it overwhelmingly powerful and rich compared to neighboring countries, a suzerainty-based Asian order came into being with China as the center and pinnacle of the "world" system. The tributary trade system was supported by the network of overseas Chinese merchants through the maritime regions of East and Southeast Asia.

The Pax Britannica that was born in Asia during the nineteenth century did not come about in a vacuum. The network of overseas Chinese, the tributary trade system, and the suzerainty-based regional order had already existed. Britain's informal empire was built on top of this preexisting order. Given this, it was only natural, indeed inevitable, that the preexisting Chinese network became so closely linked to the regional order, modern states, and free trade system that came into being in the region. It is this that forms the decisive difference between the modern international order in the West and in Asia; this, in essence, is the substance of Hamashita's argument. But is he right?

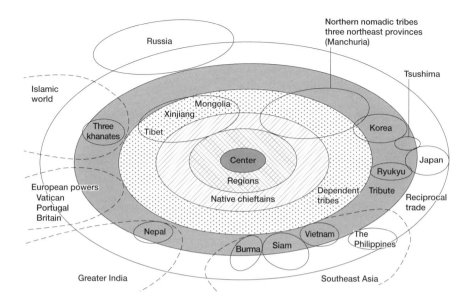

The Sinocentric regional order in Asia (after Hamashita Takeshi)

I am not convinced. A tributary trade system along the lines that Hamashita envisaged may indeed have existed until the sixteenth or seventeenth century. But by the beginning of the nineteenth century, when Raffles was in Penang and Malacca, any such system had long since gone, even though some states such as Siam kept sending missions for commercial purposes until the mid-nineteenth century. Singapore did develop as the center of the Chinese network in Southeast Asia in the nineteenth century, from the 1820s to the 1860s. But this was not because of the position of economic importance that the overseas Chinese historically occupied in the region, or because of the important role this network played in supporting the tributary trade system. A decisive change happened in the mid-nineteenth century that coincided with the development of Singapore. The alliance between Britain and the overseas Chinese came into being at the same time as the British free trade empire, and the growing economic prosperity of the overseas Chinese served British imperial interests. The overseas Chinese gained economic power, and their network expanded as Singapore developed. As a natural consequence, British free trade policy and the relationships that supported the overseas Chinese network became the twin driving principles operating within the empire.

If we were to try to construct an argument to prove this, we would have to show that by the beginning of the nineteenth century, all traces of the tributary trade system had long since disappeared, and that what existed at the time was something quite different. As a consequence, the newly constructed Pax Britannica built on the alliance between Britain and the overseas Chinese represented not a continuation of the past but a break with it. As far as Raffles is concerned, we can say that by coming to Malacca in 1811, he arrived in time to see one era draw to a close and another begin. What was the order that was ending in the region? And what meaning did this have within the context of long-term history? What did it mean for this order to fracture and for a new British-led order to take its place?

The Situation in Malacca

In 1811, Raffles proposed a new empire and called for an alliance with the Bugis. Why? As we have seen, he was well aware of the positions of economic power and influence that the Chinese and Arabs occupied in the region. His judgment was that they were the enemies of free trade. But on what grounds did he call for an alliance with the Bugis?

Of course, Raffles was not ignorant of conditions in the region. He had arrived in Penang as an employee of the East India Company in 1805, and by 1811 had become a leading specialist on "Malay" affairs. And 1811 was not the first time he had visited Malacca. He had spent several months there in 1807, and again in 1808, staying at an official government residence in the Bandar Hilir area as he recuperated from illness.

At the time, destruction was underway of the fort, official government residence, church, warehouses, prison, and other official public facilities. The fort itself had already been destroyed in 1805. In 1807, the Board of Control of the East India Company in London officially decided to destroy Malacca. The objective was to relocate the population to Penang and develop Penang as the sole commercial center in the Straits of Malacca.

Malacca would be destroyed and abandoned so that it could not be of any possible use to any other European power. This was the basic objective.

Raffles opposed this decision. During his stays in Malacca in 1807 and 1808, he visited the port and collected information from ship captains and traders about conditions in Malacca, Java, and farther afield to Bali, Celebes, and the eastern islands to the Moluccas. Based on this information, Raffles submitted a report to the governor of Penang opposing the destruction of Malacca. The report argued that even if the British destroyed Malacca, its inhabitants would not move to Penang, and neither would its trade.

Why? There were two main reasons, according to Raffles. Firstly, the nature of the population was different in Malacca and Penang. Penang was a new settlement, founded in 1786, whose inhabitants were all new arrivals from other places. They had no special feelings for Penang as a town and no fixed property. But Malacca was different. Its inhabitants had lived there for centuries. The town itself was small, with a population of just 20,000. The population was a mix of different races and religions whose ancestors had come from many different parts of the world: a small number of Europeans (mostly Dutch), Malacca-born Eurasians, Chinese, and Peranakans (the mixed-race offspring of Chinese men and local mothers), together with Malays, Portuguese, Arabs, Javanese, and Indians. Around three-quarters of this mixed population had been born in Malacca.

Many of the buildings in the town had emotional significance for the local population: mosques, churches, mausoleums, residences, and graveyards. The Chinese, for example, had lived in Malacca since before Portuguese forces captured the settlement in 1511 under the command of Alfonso Albuquerque, and for centuries their ancestors had been buried in the Chinese cemetery at Bukit Cina.

Secondly, and more importantly for the question that concerns us here, the two towns of Malacca and Penang were quite different in the nature of the trade they attracted. Malacca was a popular destination for the Bugis and other traders from the Riau and Lingga Islands and Java, as well as from Bali, Celebes, the Moluccas, and other eastern islands. Malacca was the center of the native trade of the East Indies. Penang was different. Penang was primarily a stopping point on the trade routes between India and China.

To understand what this meant, it is helpful to consider the movements of the Bugis traders. They traveled in armed sailing vessels from Macassar, Pasir, and Banjarmasin in eastern Borneo, as well as from Bali, Mandar in Celebes, and Sumbawa. Their ships would set sail from these ports at the start of the southwest monsoon, stopping off in Borneo and the north coast of Java to take on swallow nests (for bird's nest soup), spices, rice, and tobacco before arriving in the Straits of Malacca between July and October. In Malacca, they would buy cottons and opium from India. Naturally, they knew that they could obtain opium more cheaply by going to Penang. But the winds in the Straits of Malacca were notoriously unstable, particularly after September, when the northwest monsoon starts. This meant that even if the traders started north from Malacca in the direction of Penang, it was quite likely that they would have to turn back if the winds shifted on the way. For these reasons, many of the Bugis sailing vessels, particularly the smaller boats, preferred not to travel as far as Penang. Even ships that arrived in Malacca between July and October did not normally visit Penang. Bugis traders went to Malacca rather than to Penang. As a natural consequence, Malacca became the cornerstone of the Bugis trading network. This meant that even if the authorities imposed heavy duties on Malacca in an attempt to boost trade in Penang, this would not be sufficient to persuade Bugis traders to visit Penang. Instead, they would avoid Penang and Malacca altogether and visit Riau or Java instead.

This was the substance of Raffles' argument against the plans to destroy Malacca. It is clear that for Raffles, the Bugis were at the heart of the indigenous trade network within the East Indies. For him, this must have seemed self-evident. He had seen with his own eyes how the armed ships of the Bugis overwhelmingly outnumbered all the other shipping that arrived in Malacca. In the same report, Raffles writes in detail about the origins of the other traffic visiting the port: four or five ships from Borneo and Terengganu and Pahang in the eastern Malay Peninsula, carrying swallow nests, camphor, pepper, sago, and gold nuggets; ships from Java, captained by Arabs, Chinese, and Malays, laden with rice, sugar, arak, coffee, cloves, and tin; boats from the Riau and Lingga Islands close to Malacca, as well as from Palembang and Asahan on the east coast of Sumatra on the other side of the Straits of Malacca, bringing tin and pepper. But with Siak and Jambi on the east coast of Sumatra now under Dutch control, the trade with Malacca had been interrupted. Indian traders brought cottons on company ships or their own vessels from India. Three or four junks arrived from Siam (Bangkok). From China, a large junk arrived from Macao every year. The arrival of this junk energized the entire town. Boats arrived carrying produce from ports and harbors throughout the surrounding region. The Chinese brought silk, porcelain, paper, and tobacco, which they exchanged for commodities like tin, rattan, swallow nests, camphor, and pepper.

This was Malacca as Raffles painted it. Seen in this way, it is perhaps easier to understand why Raffles saw the Bugis as natural allies in his vision for a new empire in the East Indies. They occupied a paramount position in the East Indies trade centered on Malacca. Of course, this does not totally refute Hamashita's argument. In this model, the East Indies trade was merely a subsystem that was secondary to the China-based tributary trade system, and the question of who controlled this subsystem had only secondary importance for his argument. Even so, we can say for certain that by the beginning of the nineteenth century, it was no longer the Chinese but the Bugis network that played the chief role in supporting the East Indies trade. This network fanned out from its hub in Malacca, from the Straits of Malacca to the Riau and Lingga Islands, Java, Borneo, and farther afield to Bali, Celebes, the Moluccas, and other eastern islands. Raffles' idea was to make use of this network of Bugis traders to construct a new British empire in the East Indies.

The Bugis Century

The Bugis, or more accurately, the Bugis-Macassarese, emerged as the major force in the maritime regions of the East Indies between the Straits of Malacca and the Moluccas during the second half of the seventeenth century. In 1668–69, the VOC, which was then expanding its power at sea from its base in Batavia (Jakarta), formed a military alliance with the Bugis kingdoms of Bone and Soppeng in South Celebes, attacking and conquering the Macassarese kingdom of Gowa. Large numbers of the defeated Bugis and Macassarese troops spread out from Macassar to Java, as well as to Jambi and Palembang in Sumatra, and various parts of Malaya. This led to the first arrivals of Bugis-Macassarese people and their armed ships to the Straits of Malacca, as mercenaries, traders, and pirates. The Bugis ships generally carried between 40 and 80 retainers led by royal or noble "adventurers." Fleets of several dozen armed ships visited various ports of the East Indies as traders, attacking ships as pirates, hunting for slaves, and joining the forces of various Malay kings as mercenaries along the coasts of Borneo, the Riau and Lingga Islands, and the Straits of Malacca. By the middle of the eighteenth century, some of these Bugis-Macassarese adventurers set up their own kingdoms in their new homes, including the sultan of Selangor, on the west coast of Malaya where the Malaysian capital of Kuala Lumpur is located today.

But the most important event in terms of the emergence of the Bugis-Macassarese people in the Straits of Malacca took place in Riau, directly to the south of Singapore. The Riau kingdom was ruled by scions of the royal family from Malacca; in 1721, Sultan Abdul Jalil was assassinated and his throne seized. Forces led by the Bugis adventurer Daeng Merewah took Riau in the name of Sulaiman, the son of Abdul Jalil. Daeng Merewah installed Sulaiman as King of Johore, Pahang, and Riau and seized control of the kingdom with himself as vice-regent. This move established Bugis-Macassarese dominance in the Straits of Malacca. Riau became the center of a Bugis network that by then stretched from the Straits of Malacca via Borneo, South Sumatra, and Java to Celebes and the Moluccas. By the middle of the eighteenth century, Riau had become an intermediary point linking the India-China trade with the East Indies trade, visited by numerous ships from Sumatra, Java, and Borneo, as well as Bali, Celebes, the Moluccas and other islands to the east, and Siam, Cambodia, Annam, and Cochin China (Vietnam).

From their base in Riau, the Bugis took control of the seas from the Straits of Malacca to the Java Sea. By the mid-eighteenth century, Riau had 250 armed ships and some 10,000 men under arms. The VOC was unable to compete with these forces—not only in the Bugis base in the Straits of Malacca but also in South Sumatra and the Java Sea. In the mid-eighteenth century, the Company could muster a military force in Malacca of fewer than 500 men. In 1744, the governor-general of the Dutch East Indies, Gustaaf Willem van Imhoff, sent a letter of protest to Sultan Sulaiman of the kingdom of Riau. The substance of his complaint was that Bugis from Riau were trading in the ports of Borneo, Celebes, and other places without permission from the VOC—and, what was more, in recent years Bugis ships had taken to arriving on the north coast of Java to sell cottons and opium from India almost every year and were engaging in piracy close to the fort of Batavia itself; this was unacceptable, and the letter begged the sultan to do something about it.

In simple terms, therefore, in the maritime regions of the East Indies, the eighteenth century was the age of the Bugis. Their armed ships controlled the seas of the region, and Bugis merchants controlled the regional trade. During the second half of the eighteenth century, British country traders became involved in the East Indies trade through their contacts and connections with this network. The key was opium. During the 1760s, British country traders brought opium into the East Indies trade, obtaining tin in exchange. By the 1770s, the amount of tin obtained in this way by British traders was already exceeding the volumes obtained by the VOC. But this did not continue for long. In the 1780s the VOC, fearing an alliance between the British and Bugis, sent warships from the Netherlands and occupied Riau. In the mid-eighteenth century, the Bugis were not strong enough to take Malacca from Dutch control, even when Riau had a force of 10,000 men. At the end of the eighteenth century, Dutch warships took Riau, and as a result the Bugis troops who had been stationed there dispersed throughout the Straits of Malacca, South Sumatra, and various places in Borneo.

Raffles arrived in the Straits of Malacca at the end of this "Bugis century." Or, more accurately, the English East India Company established Penang just as this age was ending, seizing Malacca from the Dutch and throwing the regional order into confusion. As Raffles wrote in his report, it was the Bugis who had controlled the East Indies trade. But by this time, no one controlled the seas any longer, and piracy was rife throughout the region. For example, when the sultan of Kedah attacked the newly established settlement at Penang in 1790, around 50 warships and 1,000 men of the

Iranun people joined forces with the sultan. The Iranun were pirates from Mindanao, who normally haunted the waters around Borneo, but during this period they were active in a wider area around Southern Sumatra from Palembang to Lampung, as well as around Bangka and Belitung. The Bugis who had been chased out of Riau found employment as mercenaries with sultans in the Straits of Malacca and various parts of Borneo and used their armed ships to carry out acts of piracy in the surrounding waters. If a maharaja or great leader appeared in the maritime regions of the East Indies and united the military forces, the kingdom would prosper, and stability and prosperity would be brought to the region. But in the absence of any such maharaja, order would collapse and piracy would become rife. Lord Minto, as governor-general of the East India Company, should play the role of such a maharaja and in alliance with the Bugis establish a new empire; this was the lesson that Raffles drew from his understanding of the local history.

The Rhythm of History

What was the significance of the eighteenth-century "Bugis century" in the longer-term history of Southeast Asia? And how should we evaluate the lessons that Raffles drew from history within this wider context?

Southeast Asia has always traditionally had a much smaller population than East or South Asia. Statistics compiled by the Australian historian Anthony Reid suggest population figures for a number of areas around 1600 as follows: Siam (Thailand), 2.2 million; Malaya, 500,000; Sumatra, 2.4 million; Java, 4 million; Borneo, 670,000; Celebes, 1.2 million. Selected estimates for 1800 suggest that the population had not increased much by then: Siam, 3.5 million; Malaya, 500,000; Java, 5 million. In other words, until the mid-nineteenth century, Southeast Asia was a sparsely populated region dominated by a landscape of water and forests that stretched as far as the eye could see. The few towns were places like Malacca, Palembang, and Macassar, which had grown up as centers of the maritime and riverine trade routes. The population was otherwise concentrated in areas with fertile land, such as along the Brantas River in the interior of Central and East Java, around Mandalay in Upper Burma, and on the plains of West Sumatra, where wet-rice agriculture supported relatively dense populations.

This meant that Southeast Asia was a polycentric region, with multiple scattered centers of population built around coastal ports and pockets of fertile agricultural land. Charismatic figures with special "powers" would appear in these towns or populated regions from time to time; these figures rose to become "kings" and founded polities/states known as *negara* in Malay and *mueang* in Thai. Eventually, one of these kings would come to possess a level of power that outstripped his rivals; he would give orders to the other kings as a "maharaja" and something close to an "empire" would be formed. Oliver Wolters, the leading historian of Southeast Asia, has written extensively on this political system, particularly in Southeast Asia, which he calls the "mandala" (or "circle" of kings) model.

This political system would have been made up of something quite different from what we know as "modern states" today. I use terms like "king," "polity," "maharaja," and "empire" in quotation marks and use a roundabout paraphrase like "political system" to emphasize that all these words represent a concept quite different from what we usually think of as a "state" today.

How did they differ? The first difference is that modern states are defined by their borders. The mandala system, by contrast, was defined by centers. A great king was somewhat like a magnet. Magnetic power emanated from the great king, creating a magnetic field around him. A local order existed within each magnetic field. In the same way, an order grew up among the various kings, centered around the great king or maharaja. This was the nature of the mandala. No clearly defined borders existed within the mandala, and there was no distinction between internal affairs and foreign policy. If the "power" projected by the great king was strong, the mandala would expand; if it was weak, it would contract. And if the great king's power disappeared, the mandala too would cease to exist.

Second, the relationships that supported the mandalas, between the maharaja and the other kings, and between these kings and their vassals, were embedded in a social structure centered on kinship and marriage. In this sense, when we say that a "king" built a "polity/state" and that a "maharaja" brought other kings under his command, the "*negara*" or

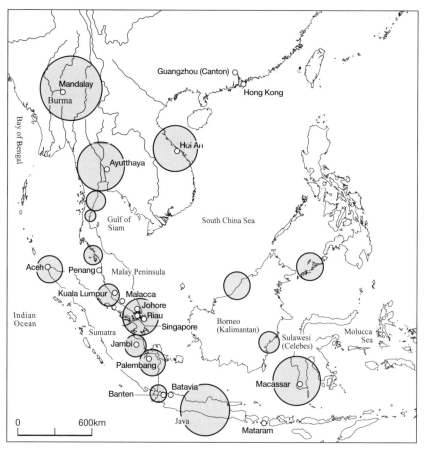

Sea- and land-based mandala states in Southeast Asia (model)

"*mueung*" we are discussing was something utterly different from the modern state as an instrument of political control. In Southeast Asia, modern states were transplanted into the region as something alien, from the outside and from above. I will have more to say about the historical significance of this later. For now, suffice it to say that at the beginning of the nineteenth century, when Raffles proposed his "new empire," modern states in the region were in their infancy; when he wrote about the "Malay kingdoms/states," he was dealing with polities that were quite different from what would be meant by these terms today.

There were essentially two types of mandala system. One of these types was the "sea mandala," such as Srivijaya, which flourished with Palembang as its royal city, occupying an important position on the maritime and riverine trade routes, or places like Malacca itself, which flourished as way stations on the long-distance trade routes that linked China, India, and the Middle East. The other type was the "land mandala," which flourished on the back of control of human resources in regions where wet-rice agriculture made large populations possible. Examples of land mandalas included places like the Mataram Sultanate around Surakarta and Yogyakarta in the interior of Central Java, and the Konbaung dynastic state in the region around Mandalay in Upper Burma.

Wolters discusses the "rhythm of history" in Southeast Asia, concentrating on the reciprocal and interacting effects of these two mandala systems. Historically, the largest market for Southeast Asia was China. And over the course of history, there was a tendency for the tributary trade to flourish when the imperial court was strong and prosperous and for private trade to become more active when the court was in decline. For example, there was a massive increase in private trade around the time of the collapse of the Yuan dynasty and the beginning of the Ming during the fourteenth century. The tributary trade took over from the time of Zheng He's voyages, until private trade became more prominent again in the sixteenth century with the decline of the Ming. When private trade was dominant, traders and merchants came freely from China to the various ports around Southeast Asia. By contrast, in the tributary trade, only countries that had been officially recognized as tribute countries could engage in trade with China, and private trade was conducted as one aspect of this. And it was Chinese traders and merchants who were actually involved in the trade. They would trade from their bases in officially recognized ports of the tributary trade. Eventually, they adopted local hairstyles and dress and became Javanese and Siamese subjects of the local kings. In the sea mandalas, the kings of the port towns managed the networks of overseas Chinese and extended their influence over the kings of neighboring ports as maharajas or great kings. Examples of centers that flourished in this way during the height of the Ming dynasty in the fifteenth century include Ayutthaya in Thailand, Pattani (now part of southern Thailand) and Malacca on the Malay Peninsula, and Gresik and Demak on the north coast of East Java.

But when the court dynasties in China declined and private trade started to expand, Chinese traders and merchants were free to travel anywhere they liked in Southeast Asia. In these circumstances, it became impossible for any single port to monopolize the China trade. The sea mandalas waned in importance. The rhythms of change in Chinese court dynasties and the rise and fall of the sea mandalas had a major impact on the reciprocal relationship between the land and sea mandalas in Southeast Asia. At times when the sea mandalas were strong and powerful, the harbor towns along the coasts were able to maintain their own autonomous footing with respect to the land mandalas. But when the sea mandalas declined and the "states" along the coastal areas split and fragmented, the land mandalas would extend their power and influence to include the coastal areas, and sometimes destroyed the coastal port towns. This is what Wolters means by the "rhythm of history" in Southeast Asia. He explains the rise and fall of Srivijaya and Malacca by reference to the rhythm of dynastic change in China, the flourishing and waning of the sea mandalas, and the competition between the sea and land mandalas in Southeast Asia.

Looked at in this way, the historical significance of the Portuguese occupation of Malacca in 1511 becomes clear. The Portuguese forces did not conquer and control the seas of the East Indies. But they blocked the formation of new sea mandalas and destroyed what Wolters described as the rhythm of history in Southeast Asia. In the sixteenth century, the Portuguese conquest of Malacca brought major changes in the political-economic map of the regions around the Straits of Malacca. Potential successor states to Malacca such as Johore at the southern tip of the Malay Peninsula, Pahang on the east coast, Aceh at the northern tip of Sumatra, and Banten in West Java, rose as new centers of trade alongside Ayutthaya in Thailand, Hoi An in Vietnam, Brunei, and Macassar.

These ports occupied strategic positions on maritime and river routes, and places like Aceh and Banten had populations of over 100,000. But none of them succeeded in creating a sea mandala to compare with previous states like Srivijaya and Malacca. This was because they could not take Malacca from the Portuguese. By the seventeenth century, VOC forces based in Batavia seized control of Malacca, Banten, and Macassar in quick succession, brought the overseas Chinese network under their influence, and further destroyed the potential for anyone else to build a new sea mandala.

The same can be said with regard to the land mandalas. Between the sixteenth and eighteenth centuries, the Portuguese and the VOC lacked sufficient power to control wide expanses of land in Southeast Asia. But just as the forces of Aceh and Johore could not take Malacca from the Portuguese, so the states of Banten in West Java, and Mataram in the interior of Central and East Java, could not take Batavia. For example, during the first half of the seventeenth century, Sultan Agung of Mataram (r. 1613–45), at the head of an army of several tens of thousands, attacked and destroyed a succession of coastal states along the north coast of Java, including Demak, Kudus, Jepara, and Surabaya. Following these campaigns, the land mandala state of Mataram gained control over Central and East Java. But it was not able to take Batavia. This was not for want of trying. In 1628–29, Sultan Agung sent a force of several tens of thousands to attack Batavia. However, this effort was unsuccessful. The logistics of the Mataram army were dependent on boats, which were destroyed by the VOC navy.

This was the decisive difference between Southeast Asia and East Asia. In East Asia, Japan adopted a policy of *sakoku* (isolation) in 1635, and China introduced a similar "closed seas" policy beginning in the second half of the seventeenth century, after Zheng Chenggong (Koxinga) had driven the Dutch forces from Formosa (Taiwan). This meant that East Asia was shut off to the outside world under the hegemony of early modern states. This was probably the major reason for the survival of the tributary trade system into the nineteenth century in China's vicinities. In Southeast Asia, by contrast, neither the sea- nor the land-based mandala states were able to expel either the Portuguese or the VOC. As a result, Southeast Asia was not closed to the outside world. It was not possible to close it off. But the Portuguese and Dutch forces did not bring a new order to Southeast Asia. Instead, these new powers dismantled the distinctive order that had existed in Southeast Asia and threw the region into disorder. The tributary trade system largely came to an end at this time in Southeast Asia. The overseas Chinese network was torn apart. The power of the Bugis, who traveled the seas of the region in their armed ships, as mercenaries, traders, and pirates, was in this sense the natural consequence of this era of confusion.

When we look at history from this perspective, we can comprehend the significance of Raffles' perceiving Malacca at the start of the nineteenth century to be at the end of one era and the beginning of a new one. His idea was to bring the era of chaos and confusion in the East Indies to an end and to build a British free trade empire by having the Bugis establish a new sea-based mandala state. But after Java was handed back to the Dutch, and Macassar and Riau were under Dutch control, it became clear that the Bugis did not have the power to build a sea-based mandala state. For the "adventurers" without the power to build a kingdom, there was no choice but to become "pirates." And piracy did not suit the needs of the East India Company at all. With the establishment of a British free trade empire, the age of chaos came to an end and the modern age began. The rhythm of history was soon forgotten, and a new leviathan emerged to take the place of the mandalas.

CHAPTER THREE

Toddling Leviathans

Singapore was "founded" by Raffles in 1819 and incorporated a few years later into the new Straits Settlements colony together with Penang and Malacca in 1826. The Straits Settlements formed the core of the nineteenth-century British free trade empire. The three Straits Settlements were the only places where the East India Company established local government offices and ruled directly. But from here, British power was projected into the surrounding region. From their bases in the Straits Settlements, British ships patrolled the Straits of Malacca and the South China Sea, while a network of Chinese secret societies fanned out like a coral reef across the Malay Peninsula, the east coast of Sumatra, and the Riau Archipelago.

This was Britain's informal empire. The two states that exist in this region today, Singapore and Malaysia, were born out of the Straits Settlements and took their first toddling steps during the formative period of this informal empire. Early states in the Dutch East Indies, the Philippines, and the Chakri dynastic state also began to change at this time in response to the formation of the British free trade empire, eventually becoming the states we know today as Indonesia, the Philippines, and Thailand.

The term "leviathan" is often used as a metaphor for the modern state. When discussing modern states, we tend to think automatically of sovereign states as we know them today, as defined by Max Weber, with all their trappings of might and majesty. But even the most impressively dignified state started from more humble beginnings. In what follows, I propose to look at how Singapore, Malaysia, Indonesia, the Philippines, and Thailand began their toddling growth as modern states and transformed into the leviathans we know today.

Defining the Modern State

The term "state" is a convenient one, but like the concepts of "culture" and "society," it is not easy to define in simple terms. A "state" is a highly abstract concept, a little bit like the term "vehicle." If we define "vehicle" as "a means by which a person moves through space without using his or her own feet," our definition would encompass everything from piggyback rides to palanquins to space shuttles. The concept of "state" is the same: if we define it as a "system of control," then the category would include everything from the ancient Japanese state to the mandala states of Southeast Asia, the Roman empire, and modern nation-states. I am not suggesting that nothing meaningful can be said about "states" on this general level. But that is not our purpose here. Today's Southeast Asia includes states like Thailand, the Philippines, and Singapore. Each of these has its own distinctive qualities, but nevertheless, we know as soon as we look at them that we are dealing with a "state." Why do we react in this way? What is it that tells us that what we are looking at is a "state"? What characteristics do states have in common?

In his memoirs, the first prime minister of Burma, U Nu, compared the state he inherited from the British to a car:

> He had no special bent for administrative work, no experience whatsoever . . . Thakin Nu saw before him a derelict, with leaks in its gas tank and radiator, and punctures in front and rear tyres. He, who had never learnt to drive and had seen a motor car only once or twice at a distance, was expected to take the wheel and drive it over the worst road imaginable.

In the same spirit, S. Rajaratnam, former foreign minister of Singapore, compared his country to a supersonic jet fighter: "as automated as possible with back-up and fail-safe devices, but requiring a trained pilot to show its full range." And that, claimed Rajaratnam, was why Singapore needed Lee Kwan Yew.

We can define the modern state as a machine or instrument of control. A state is different from a nation. If a nation is an "imagined community," or something that exists only in people's hearts and minds, then a state is a sociological structure with real substance: a system and a machine, like a church, university, or corporation. As Benedict Anderson tells us, a state has its own staff, who "enter" the machinery of state based on rules according to age, education, and sex, and eventually "leave" again. A state also has its own memory and possesses the motives of self-preservation and self-aggrandizement.

In Southeast Asia, the modern state as a machine or instrument of rule of this kind was born in the nineteenth century, during the time of the British free trade empire. It did not spring into existence spontaneously. It was brought in from the outside, as something alien. To understand how different these modern states were from what had gone before, it is enough to compare these newborn leviathans with the distinctive political system that had grown up spontaneously in the region, which Wolters referred to as the "mandala" states system.

We looked at the mandala states in the previous chapter. Historically, the Southeast Asian region was made up of numerous centers. From time to time, a person with an unusual degree of power would rise to prominence in a settlement that controlled a strategic position along a transport route or in an area with a concentrated population. That person might become a "king" and form a "polity/state" known as *negara* in Malay or *mueang* in Thai. A mandala was formed when a "great king" or maharaja emerged who could command the allegiance of several of these regional "kings." This meant that a mandala had no borders; it was defined by its center. The king, with his court and capital, was the center of the world; the order of the mandala represented the order of the world itself. The mandala states were supported by relationships of power and allegiance; these were embedded in turn into a social structure built around relationships of kinship and marriage. The mandalas were supported by these other social institutions and were not organized around separate principles of their own. Another important point is that the mandalas had neither the intention nor the ability to enforce total and systematic rule over the lives of the populations under their control. As a classical Javanese source phrased it, the whole populace could be likened to a forest, and the king to a tiger. Although the mandalas gave meaning and a rationale to the existing order, they did not have a profound influence on people's daily lives.

A few simple comparisons will suffice to make clear just how different these mandalas were from the "leviathan" states, compared to automobiles and jet fighters in the descriptions above. Unlike the mandala states, which were embedded in local social structures, modern states as machines and instruments of control were alien species that were transplanted into Southeast Asia from outside and imposed from above. Unlike the network of kinship and marriage relationships that formed the state system in the mandalas, the people who staff a modern state are recruited as civil servants by principles quite unconnected with existing social structures. In addition, modern states have endeavored to attain total mastery of the territories and populations under their control by means of new "technologies" such as laws, maps, population and land registers, and trade statistics. Whereas the mandalas were defined by their centers, the territory of modern states is defined by borders, and the power of the state applies equally and without differentiation to everything inside this clearly defined territory. And whereas the mandalas served to give meaning to the existing world order, the modern states had no rationale for their existence, just as a car, to borrow U Nu's metaphor, cannot have any ontological meaning.

Modern states of this kind first arrived and started their toddling existences in Southeast Asia. What paths did they follow as they grew? What was destroyed by these states, and what new things did they bring with them?

The Straits Settlements State

Let us begin our discussion with the Straits Settlements, which eventually became the modern states of Singapore and Malaysia. Defining precisely when this state was born is not easy. But we can say with reasonable certainty that it took its first steps following the founding of Penang (1786) and Singapore (1819) and their combination with Malacca into the Straits Settlements in 1826.

This was not a sovereign but a colonial state. At first, the Straits Settlements were under the authority of the East India Company, but they were transferred to direct government control under the India Office in

London following the dissolution of the Company in 1858 and under the Colonial Office after 1867.

The Straits Settlements were an example of a small state—or, to use a more familiar phrase, "small government." When the three settlements were brought together under unified control as a single colony, the colonial government was made up of just 14 members, including a president or governor and three councilors, as well as approximately 60 supernumerary officials. The armed forces of the colony comprised 17 European artillerymen and 30 soldiers of the Madras infantry, as well as a steam-powered warship and two government sail-powered ships. This did not change substantially even after 1867, when responsibility for the Settlements was transferred to the Colonial Office. In that year, the government was still made up of 14 full members of staff and 306 supernumerary employees. Nevertheless, this was a full-fledged state. The government was headed by a governor and comprised a colonial secretary, attorney general, bureau of revenue, treasurer, and auditor general, as well an army and navy, and three councilors respectively responsible for the affairs of Singapore, Malacca, and Penang.

As the center of the British free trade empire in Southeast Asia, the Straits Settlements developed as a collection of free ports. But a free port derives no income from duties—and even the smallest state requires money to cover payroll and other expenses. The Straits Settlements state raised the money it needed from the economic activities of the Chinese. In Singapore, this mostly involved pepper and gambier plantations. Revenue farming, principally on opium, was the means that made this possible. The "respectable" Chinese who had won the trust of the British entered into a bidding process to obtain rights to a monopoly to sell opium. The Chinese secret societies became subcontractors, selling opium to the coolies who worked on the pepper and gambier plantations. The government obtained more than 50 percent of its revenue from this system.

John Crawfurd, a colleague of Raffles who helped establish the economic foundations of Singapore, said that he considered "one Chinaman equal in value . . . of two natives of the Coromandel coast and to four Malays at least." This estimation, of course, was based on their value to the state. In accordance with these views, the Straits Settlements government actively encouraged large-scale immigration from China. In turn, this helped to ensure the prosperity of the British free trade empire. In 1819, for example, there were 20 pepper and gambier plantations in Singapore. By 1839, this number had increased to 350, and to 600 by 1848. These plantations also expanded around this time across the Straits to Johore, on the Malay Peninsula. Throughout the nineteenth century, some tens of thousands—and at times hundreds of thousands—of Chinese moved into the Straits Settlements every year. Of course, not all of them settled permanently. Probably four out of every five returned to their native villages after working in the colony for a certain length of time. Nevertheless, this massive influx of Chinese workers led to the expansion of the pepper and gambier plantations and the development of tin mines. As industry boomed, the Chinese network spread from the Straits Settlements to surrounding areas in the Malay Peninsula, the Riau Archipelago, and the east coast of Sumatra.

But this expansion also brought serious problems. Every year, huge numbers of Chinese people would arrive in the Straits Settlements from Fujian and Guangdong Provinces, and spread out from there to surrounding regions. This helped the economy to prosper and increased the revenue of the Straits Settlements government. In itself, of course, this was something to be welcomed. But despite the tendency to refer to the "Chinese" as if they were a monolithic group, in fact the migrants spoke different languages and brought quite different customs with them, depending on what part of China they were from. Many were affiliated with secret societies such as the Ghee Hin Society, the Hai San Society, and the Tua Pek Kong Association, which were societies engaged in a constant battle for control of the opium monopolies and the rights to tin mining.

This meant that to control the Chinese network, it was not enough simply to channel money from Chinese economic activities by farming out the right to sell opium and other controlled substances. It was also necessary at times to subdue the secret societies by means of real force, to expel powerful members of the secret societies from the colony, and to establish state authority on a firm basis.

This was not straightforward. Until the mid-1860s, there was not a single British official in the Straits Settlements government who understood Chinese (or, more accurately, Hokkien, Cantonese, Teochew, Hakka, or Hainanese). And in the mid-nineteenth century, as even the head of the Singapore police admitted, it was simply not possible to control the secret societies with the limited powers available. But violence among the secret societies happened only intermittently in the Straits Settlements. A more serious problem concerned the atoll-like territories of the informal empire in the surrounding areas. As the stream of Chinese immigrants continued, the scope of their economic activities expanded beyond the Straits Settlements to the Malay Peninsula, the Riau Archipelago, and the east coast of Sumatra. The "Malay kings" in these areas tried to bring the Chinese network under their control as the Straits Settlements state had done. But they found they could not—and this led to problems.

The Malay kings were facing a period of transition at this time. In the 1820s, around the time when the Straits Settlements were incorporated into a single colony, the suppression of piracy became a serious issue, and by the mid-1830s, steam-powered warships were available in the Straits Settlements. These were highly effective in suppressing piracy in an age still dominated by sail. Around the same time, an agreement was reached between the Straits Settlements government and the government of the Dutch East Indies to cooperate in an effort to wipe out hotbeds of piracy in the region. By the 1840s, piracy had been eradicated from the seas around the Straits Settlements. The era in which the Malays, Bugis, and Iranun traders, pirates, and mercenaries had sailed in armed ships throughout the Straits of Malacca, the South China Sea, and the wider East Indies came to an end.

By the middle of the nineteenth century, the Bugis adventurers, Iranun pirates, and Malay kings found themselves stranded like fish out of water. But a new opportunity was about to present itself. This was the development of tin mining in places like Perak and Selangor on the west coast of the Malay Peninsula and the growth of pepper and gambier plantations in Johore, across the Straits from Singapore. The Malays, Bugis, and Iranun were not themselves directly involved in developing the tin mines or managing the plantations. This work was the responsibility of the Chinese.

Image from *The Expedition to Borneo of H.M.S. Dido for the Suppression of Piracy: With Extracts from the Journal of J. Brooke Esq., of Sarawak*, p. 471 (Archivad/Alamy Stock Photo)

British country traders in Singapore and Penang supplied the funding together with their Chinese partners. The bosses of Chinese secret societies such as the Ghee Hin Society and Hai San Society raised the materials and manpower for development of the mines, and owners developed the mines using Chinese coolie labor. The Malay kings and Bugis adventurers provided areas for tin mines to capitalists from the Straits Settlements and the Chinese secret societies and, following the example of the Straits Settlements government, let them take charge of opium, alcohol, and gambling. The Chinese secret societies then squeezed money out of the Chinese coolies by farming out tariff rights. This was the normal pattern.

From this perspective, it is not surprising that the British and Chinese capitalists, the secret societies, Malay kings, Bugis adventurers, and others should occasionally come to blows over the right to control the tin mines. Dynastic disputes were a frequent trigger of these clashes.

To avoid misunderstanding, it is worth noting that in the mid-nineteenth century, the "native" population of the "kingdoms" of Perak and Selangor was only around 20,000 or 30,000. The power of the so-called "kings" was therefore somewhat limited. Nevertheless, theoretically, these "kings" were the owners of the areas where the tin mines were located, and the sovereigns of the "kingdoms." Whenever a dispute arose over succession, the Malay kings, Bugis adventurers, and Iranun mercenaries would each put forward their own candidate and fight for supremacy, while capitalists and secret societies from the Straits Settlements offered financial and military support.

During the 1850s and 1860s, order collapsed in the royal kingdoms of Perak and Selangor and other kingdoms on the west coast of the Malay Peninsula. These civil disturbances in regions close to the British free trade empire threatened the order and stability of the Straits Settlements. In the 1870s, this led the Straits Settlements government to intervene in the Malay kingdoms, bringing about a transformation as the informal zone of free trade influence was incorporated into the formal empire.

When the British intervened, they generally sent a resident official and introduced a police force to restore law and order, then seized the king's rights to farm out the rights to the trade in opium and other commodities, took control of the treasury, and generally set to work building up the leviathan. The Straits Settlements government did all of this in the name of the "Malay kings" (the rajas of Perak, Selangor, and the other surrounding kingdoms). By this time, the Chinese population of the west coast of the Malay Peninsula already outnumbered the native Malays. Nevertheless, the fiction was maintained that these were "Malay" kingdoms. Later, with independence and the birth of modern Malaysia, this became the most important justification for the policy of preferential treatment of the Malay population. But that still lay far in the future. The most important facts for our discussion at this stage are that the influx of Chinese immigrants was the key to the economic prosperity of the region and that the toddling leviathan of the Straits Settlements government was responsible for controlling the Chinese and guaranteeing British hegemony.

The Dutch East Indies State

The rise of the British free trade empire with its center in the Straits Settlements colony brought profound changes to the political and economic order in Southeast Asia. None of the surrounding states—the Dutch East Indies based in Batavia, the Philippine state with its capital at Manila, or the Chakri dynastic state in Bangkok—could challenge the newly established British hegemony. But this did not mean that they were happy to accept it, or British ideas of free trade, without reservations. The question of how to react to the rise of the new British empire and its free trade policy was the major issue facing these states in the middle of the nineteenth century. Between the 1820s and the 1860s, the response to this challenge transformed the Dutch East Indies, the Spanish colony of the Philippines, and the Chakri dynasty in Siam (later, Thailand—for more on this, see Chapter 7) into modern states. In this chapter, I propose to look at two of these cases, the Dutch East Indies and the Philippines.

Let us begin with the Dutch East Indies—the predecessor to today's Republic of Indonesia. This state was born much earlier than the British Straits Settlements, at the beginning of the seventeenth century, when Jan Pieterszoon Coen established a VOC base in Jayakarta, which was renamed Batavia. The Dutch East Indies therefore came into being around the same time as the Tokugawa shogunate in Edo (Tokyo) in Japan. Like the Tokugawa shogunate, the VOC government was not a modern state. The VOC-ruled Dutch East Indies was one of several "company states" that, despite their official status as companies, acted as states in many parts of the West and East Indies from the seventeenth to the nineteenth centuries. But the VOC went bankrupt at the end of the eighteenth century, and the East Indies were placed under British control at the beginning of the 1810s. It was after Java was returned to Dutch control in the mid-1810s that the state began its gradual transformation into a modern leviathan.

But the environment in which the Dutch East Indies state developed was quite different from the one in which the Straits Settlements grew. The Straits Settlements had only a marginal significance for Britain. So long as the government of the Settlements did not incur a serious fiscal burden for the East India Company (or the British government, after 1867), it was relatively free to do as it liked. By contrast, Java was the most important Dutch colony. The prosperity and prestige of the home country depended on what happened in Java, and the management of the colony was regularly a major point of contention in Dutch politics. This was particularly true of the period between Java's return to Dutch control in the mid-1810s and the early 1830s—a time when the Netherlands was still suffering the deleterious effects of occupation during the Napoleonic Wars. This economic crisis became even more severe after the industrial regions of Belgium broke away and became independent in 1830. The question of how to make Java profitable was the biggest issue in Dutch politics at the time.

What were the options? The Dutch had little to gain by accepting the British free trade system. Of the 171 large ships that arrived in Batavia in 1819, the year in which Singapore was "founded," for example, 62 were British and 50 were from the United States. Only 19 were Dutch ships. During the 1810s and 1820s, the East Indies state ran a fiscal deficit and was in debt to British commercial firms. If the East Indies adopted the British free trade model in these circumstances, it was likely to be only a matter of time before Java came under the control of the British country traders and their Chinese allies. What could be done to ensure that this did not happen and to make sure that Java became profitable for the Netherlands? This was the essential question facing the Dutch government and the government of the Dutch East Indies.

It was under these conditions that the Dutch decided on their basic approach to management of the East Indies. If they could not compete with Britain in free trade, the only alternative was protectionism. Unlike the Straits Settlements, Java was blessed with rich fertile land and a large population. By 1800, there were already some five million people in Java. The Dutch state controlled the entire territory of Java and forced farmers to work the lands as a form of corvée, cultivating tropical cash crops like sugar, indigo, and tobacco for the European market. The Dutch royal trading company then had a monopoly on sales of these products in Europe. The system was founded on forced cultivation and trade monopolies. Luckily, the Netherlands enjoyed a central occupation within Western Europe, so that selling the produce was not difficult. The difficulties all lay on the production side. To transform Java into a huge state-controlled plantation and force farmers to grow tropical cash crops required a powerful state machine. But sending Dutchmen from home and staffing the government entirely with white Europeans made no financial sense. The Dutch decided to appoint the Javanese nobility as government officials and introduced a commission system whereby prices were decided according to the volume of cash crops produced. A small number of Europeans were placed in strategic positions within the machinery of government (fewer than 200 in the mid-nineteenth century) to ensure that the state functioned according to the wishes of the East Indies government, with the governor-general at its head. The basic model of the Dutch East Indies state (and later the Republic of Indonesia) was now in place.

The government of the Dutch East Indies also introduced a system for farming out monopoly rights on opium and other products around this time. From the 1830s to the 1870s, income from these sources made up around 30 percent of the government's total revenue. In fact, this was not the first time that such a system had been introduced in Java. Revenue farming already made up an important source of income for the Dutch East Indies state in the seventeenth century, and the same model was adopted by the Mataram that ruled the inland areas of Central Java, with its centers in Yogyakarta and Surakarta. But revenue farming as it was used in the nineteenth century was something quite different. In the seventeenth and eighteenth centuries, those involved most were market revenue contractors and commissions on customs duties. By contrast, the opium farming was based on the model used in the Straits Settlements. Essentially, it worked in the same way. The government imported opium from India. An open bidding process was then carried out in each administrative region for the right to a monopoly on the sale of opium—normally for a period of three years. The contracts went almost exclusively to Chinese, who paid monthly contract fees and sold the opium.

But there were two differences with the British model. First, in the Straits Settlements, Chinese immigrants were the foundation of the economy. The question was how to extract money from them. Consequently, opium was sold through the Chinese secret society network to Chinese coolies who worked in the tin mines and on the pepper and gambier plantations. By contrast, the economic foundations of the Dutch East Indies were the Javanese farmers, and it was to them that the opium was sold. The Chinese secret society network could not be used directly as a network to sell opium. Instead, "respectable" Chinese who had lived in Java for generations and enjoyed the trust of the Dutch became contractors with the right to sell opium. More than 10,000 opium dens were established throughout Java, in addition to which Javanese and Chinese traders traveled from village to village selling opium on credit.

Second, the government in the East Indies set the wholesale price of opium imported from India at two to four times the level of the sales price in the Straits Settlements. Naturally, this led to smuggling on a large scale. According to the estimates of the East Indies government, opium equivalent in volume to almost the entire government supply was smuggled from Singapore to Java via Buleleng, in Bali. The success or failure of a person who acquired opium farming rights therefore depended on whether the contractor could eradicate opium smugglers and could maintain his monopoly of the market, by doing the smuggling himself if necessary. For this reason, opium farm contractors used their close relationships with the native bureaucracy (i.e., the local nobility), headed by the regents, to control the local toughs who were present in the markets, gambling places, opium dens, and brothels, occasionally serving as minions to the native officials, and used them as police and spies to clamp down on the sale of smuggled opium. Of course, this came at a cost. The Javanese bureaucrats and local toughs were free to demand extortionate fees from the opium revenue farmers in return. By paying this protection money, the opium revenue farmers obtained a monopoly over the market. The need to eradicate smuggled opium also provided the ideal excuse for the opium revenue farmers to try to exclude their competitors from local village markets and to gather rice and other produce from Javanese farmers through the sale of opium on credit. In simple terms, this meant that an alliance grew between the Javanese nobility and the Chinese, who increasingly came to control the Javanese rural economy. These developments coincided with the growth of the Dutch East Indies state into a leviathan during the nineteenth century.

In the British Straits Settlements, the Chinese network was closely linked to the underbelly of the state. But in the Dutch East Indies state, the

Group of Chinese gamblers in a gambling den, 1880s (Courtesy of the National Archives of Singapore)

Dutch-dominated state machine ruled via a network of native bureaucrats and the Chinese network. Further down, this machinery of power was deeply implicated in a "twilight zone" between the legal and illegal worlds, inhabited by traveling merchants, local toughs, gamblers, and prostitutes. I will have more to say later about how the government of the Dutch East Indies worked to restructure this twilight zone at the beginning of the twentieth century in the name of the "white man's burden," as they tried to encourage the continuing modernization of the developing leviathan. For now, we should note that this condition, in which the institutions of state were sunk into an unruly and insalubrious twilight zone, was not peculiar to the nineteenth-century Dutch East Indies. The circumstances have not changed much, even today. And this should not surprise us, since the foundations of the Dutch East Indies state (and today's Indonesia, to some extent) are built on control of Javanese farmers.

The Philippines

What about the toddling state in the Philippines?

From the middle of the sixteenth until the end of the nineteenth centuries, the Philippines were under Spanish control. The history of the Philippines as a state therefore goes back even farther than that of the Dutch East Indies. However, the Philippines did not make a smooth transition into a leviathan during the nineteenth century in the way the Dutch East Indies did. This is one of the major reasons why the Dutch East Indies grew into a strong state while the Philippines remained weak. To a considerable extent, this was due to the environment in which the Philippines developed as a state.

There were two major turning points in the history of the Philippine state during the Spanish period. The first was the British occupation of Manila (1762–64) during the Seven Years' War (1756–63). This came as a huge shock to Spain. To rebuild a unified system of governance after regaining control, Spain adopted a new economic policy based on the models of the VOC and the English East India Company. A system of forced cultivation of tobacco was introduced together with a state monopoly, and the Royal Company of the Philippines was established. Attempts were also made to grow coffee, cotton, and other cash crops and to develop mining and revenue farming based on tariffs on opium and other substances. Tobacco was the only one of these to succeed.

The other major turning point was Mexican independence. From the sixteenth century until the 1820s, the galleon trade linking Mexico and China, with the Philippines as an intermediary point, had brought large profits to the Spanish in Manila; with Mexican independence, this came to an end, together with the subsidy previously paid from Mexico to the Philippine government. The Philippines was on the periphery of the Spanish empire. But as the empire in the Americas passed into history, Spain was forced to do whatever it could to try to make the Philippines pay. What were the options? Like the government of the Dutch East Indies, the state in the Philippines faced this question as the British free trade empire took form in Southeast Asia.

The answer the Dutch East Indies government reached involved forced cultivation, trade monopolies, and revenue farming. This led to the development of a leviathan that gorged itself on Javanese farmers. The government of the Philippines came up with a different response. Or, to put it more accurately, the government did not adopt a model based on forced cultivation, trade monopolies, and revenue farming. These had been tried without success in the Philippines in the second half of the eighteenth century. There were at least two reasons that the government of the Philippines did not try to copy the Dutch response.

First, in the Philippines the Catholic church held significant sway in regional government. Regional administration was organized into provinces, towns, and villages. The central plaza of every town was dominated by a church alongside a town hall or similar government office. The mayor was elected by the local population, but the parish priests were all Spaniards. And the priests were involved in the government of the town. The register of taxpayers required the approval of the parish priest before it could be finalized, and the presence and recommendation of the parish priest was necessary for the selection of a mayor. This meant that any attempt to improve or strengthen the machinery of state was immediately resisted by the Church.

Another problem distinctive to the Philippines was the presence of the mestizo (mixed-race) population. In Java, the children of Chinese men and local women continued to be regarded as Chinese, regardless of how assimilated they may have been culturally. They lived in Chinese districts and were legally required to wear Chinese dress and hairstyles. In the Philippines, however, the offspring of Chinese men and local women became mestizos. The Spanish brought the legal concept of the mestizo with them from Latin America. This meant that the large numbers of Chinese people arriving in the Philippines became mestizos within a generation or two, owning land and putting down roots in various places in the Philippines. What would happen if a system of revenue farming were introduced in these circumstances? It was likely that the supposedly "Chinese" revenue farmers would become mestizos within the space of a generation or two and turn their economic power into political influence. And this was too risky to be allowed.

What were the alternatives? If forced cultivation, trade monopolies, and revenue farming were not the answer, then the only remaining option would be free trade. The basic answer was to open the Philippine economy to British country traders and their Chinese allies and let the Philippines thrive on the revenue that came in from duties. Manila therefore officially became an open port in 1834. I say "officially" because, in fact, a blind eye had been turned to trade in Manila since the end of the eighteenth century—a British trading house had even been built in Manila in 1809. This system was further refined in the 1850s. In 1850, for example, a law was introduced to encourage Chinese immigration, and in 1855 the ports of Iloilo, Zamboanga, and Sual were opened, followed by Cebu in 1860.

In economic terms, this policy had the expected results. The economy of the Philippines was incorporated into the British free trade empire centered on Singapore and Hong Kong, and the Philippine trade came under the control of British traders and their Chinese allies. More important for our present discussion is the significance this had on the political-economic situation within the country. At the time, transportation links between the open ports and rural villages largely depended on the traders, wholesalers, and regional merchants who operated in the open ports.

Ikehata Setsuho describes these regional merchants as follows:

> The regional traders normally lived in large towns situated at important points on the transportation network, and traveled around the regular markets that took place on given days of the week in the surrounding market towns, selling their produce. They often sold on credit, in return for a promise of agricultural produce; since in many cases they were also the buyers for agricultural produce for export, this was an effective way to make sure that they would be able to obtain what they wanted come harvest time. For the same reasons, buyers were happy to grant loans and advances to farmers on request. When harvest time arrived, regional traders would travel by river on their small boats or overland by oxcart to buy and collect sugar, manila hemp, indigo, rice, and other produce. In cases of natural disaster, locust plagues, or other adverse conditions affecting the harvest, farmers often struggled to pay back advances or provide the goods they had already been paid for. It was from these farmers' debts . . . that traders and usurious moneylenders became concentrated on the land.

Until the middle of the nineteenth century, many of these regional merchants were mestizos. This was a consequence of Philippine government policy. During the mid-eighteenth century, the Philippine government passed three separate Chinese expulsion laws. As a result, the Chinese population decreased dramatically, and those that remained were restricted to Manila and its environs. Chinese economic activity in the provinces declined, and the mestizos and a small number of "native" merchants stepped in to fill the gap. But the situation changed again rapidly after the port of Manila was opened to international trade. The Philippine government now welcomed Chinese immigrants, and the Chinese were allowed considerable freedom to settle and move around the country as they liked. In the 1850s, Chinese traders began to move into the provincial trade again. The mestizos switched to extending high-interest loans to regional traders, land ownership, and growing produce for export. By the end of the nineteenth century, a new Filipino elite emerged from this landed mestizo class and began to challenge Spanish rule. This too was in part the natural consequence of the fact that the Philippine state had remained an underdeveloped leviathan for most of the nineteenth century.

In this way, numerous leviathans began to appear in Southeast Asia during the nineteenth century, each one different in terms of both the conditions in which it emerged and its individual characteristics. Chronologically speaking, these states came into existence just before Japan started to construct a leviathan of its own in the form of the Meiji state. As modern states—as machines or instruments of control—these Southeast Asian states did not differ greatly from the Meiji state. But they were different in terms of their models and their ontological significance. The Meiji state was built on the model of the nation-states of the European "powers" but represented a Japanese state attempt to shape the people into a modern nation in a top-down fashion on its own account. By contrast, the states in Southeast Asia were colonial states, which took their models from one another. This meant that the modern age arrived in Southeast Asia and Japan in different forms.

CHAPTER FOUR

The Formation of Plural Societies

Today, words like "Japanese," "Chinese," "Malay," "Dutch," and "Filipino" have a fairly stable meaning for us, describing well-defined national or ethnic groups. This was not yet the case in the nineteenth century. For example, in his letter to Lord Minto, Raffles referred to the "Malays" as follows:

> The tribes of which they are composed, though varying radically in customs, manners, religion, and language, and possessing very different degrees of civilization, have long been confounded by Europeans under the general appellation of Malays, a term which may still be retained for convenience.

That same year, having captured Java for the British, Lord Minto wrote to his wife from Batavia, describing the "Dutch" women he had encountered among the upper classes in Batavia who spoke no language but Malay:

> The Dutch did not encourage, nor indeed allow freely, European women to go out to their colonies in India. The consequence has been that the men lived with native women, whose daughters, gradually borrowing something from the father's side, and becoming a mixed breed, are now the wives and of rank and fashion in Java . . . Their education is almost wholly neglected; or rather no means exist to provide for it. They are attended from their cradles by numerous slaves, by whom they are trained in helplessness and laziness; and from such companions and governesses, you may conceive how much accomplishment or refinement in manners or opinions they are likely to acquire.

For Raffles and Minto, words like "Malay" and "Dutch" held a precise and clearly understood meaning. But what about the people who were referred to in these passages I have just quoted: to what extent would these terms have been meaningful for them? The "Dutch" women who had been "attended from their cradles by numerous slaves" would probably not understand why Lord Minto took such a critical view of them, and most of the people that Raffles and his fellow Europeans referred to "for convenience" as Malays certainly did not think of themselves as "Malay" at all.

However, this situation was to change dramatically over the course of the following century, as words like "Malay," "Chinese," and "Dutch" came to have stable meanings close to the sense in which we still use them today.

What happened to cause this change, and how? What were the processes that started around this time? How did people define themselves before ethnic/racial categories ("I am Dutch;" "I am a Malay") came to hold identity hostage?

The Case of Abdullah the Munshi

One useful guide in attempting to answer these questions is the *Hikayat Abdullah* (Life of Abdullah), a memoir written by Abdullah bin Abdul Kadir in the middle of the nineteenth century. We have encountered Abdullah already, when we looked at his description of Raffles as he knew him in Malacca. Abdullah wrote his book in Malay; the quotations that follow are from the English translation by A.H. Hill.

Abdullah was born in Malacca in 1797. He moved from Malacca to Singapore in 1819, not long after the "founding" of the settlement, and died in 1854 in Jeddah while on a pilgrimage to Mecca. In 1810, at the age of 13, he was employed by Raffles and was the youngest of the scribes working under him around the time he wrote his proposal for a new British empire in Southeast Asia. Abdullah's dealings with Europeans date from around this time. Later, when the first mission school was opened in Malacca in 1815, he got a job teaching the missionaries Malay and spent the rest of his life as a teacher of that language. His memoir was written in response to a suggestion from a "friend of mine, an Englishman [*orang putih*: literally, "white person"] of whom I was fond." The book was completed in 1843 and published in 1849. It was the first autobiography written in Malay.

Traditionally, the first step in any autobiography or memoir is for the writer to introduce himself. The first-person narrator is introduced as a well-defined personality, and then he narrates how he has grown to become the person he is today. This is the general format of most autobiographies. How does Abdullah introduce himself in his memoir?

In the opening passages of the book, Abdullah writes as follows:

> My great-grandfather was an Arab from Yemen, of the family of Othman, whose name was Shaikh Abdul Kadir. He was a teacher of religion and language. He left Yemen and went to the State of Nagur in Kalinga, where he taught the people for a long time. He married there and had four sons . . . After his death his children travelled to the East. [One of them,] Mohamed Ibrahim, came to Malacca and married my grandmother whose name was Peri Achi, the daughter of Shaikh Mira Lebai. When my father was born, he was called Abdul-Kadir so that he might carry the blessing of his grandfather's name.

The narrator's father, Shaikh Abdul Kadir, grew up in Malacca, where he worked as a merchant and religious instructor, teaching the Koran and Islamic prayers. He also worked as a scribe and amanuensis in Malay, writing contracts and letters for Malay rajas.

Shaikh Abdul Kadir was married in Malacca in 1785, or 1200 by the Islamic calendar. "My mother's father was an Indian from Kedah who had embraced the Muslim faith, and moved to Malacca where my mother, whose name was Selamah, was born." Abdullah was therefore the direct offspring of these two people, Shaikh Abdul Kadir and Selamah. His self-introduction continues as follows.

Next, he speaks of the origins of his name.

His mother lost four children before he was born, all of them dead in childhood. The grief caused his mother almost to lose her mind, and she wept constantly. "There came to Malacca an Arab Sayid named Habib Abdullah, of the Haddad family; he was a saintly man held in the highest regard by the people of Malacca." This man told Abdullah's mother that if it should please God to give her another son, she should give the child his name. And so, when the child was born in due course, he was given the name Abdullah.

Next, he writes about his upbringing.

He was born and grew up in Kampong Pali, "pali" being the Tamil word for mosque. The child's paternal grandmother ran a religious Islamic school at Kampong Pali, where some 200 boys and girls learnt the Koran. "I was the darling of my grandmother who used to sit me down next to her while she was teaching. . . . From early morning until six o' clock in the evening no sound was heard but the chanting of the Koran."

Abdullah grows up with the sound of recitations of the Koran in his ears. Then he begins his own studies of the Koran. And one day, when his studies are nearly complete:

> For a few days longer my father made me go over my reading again, perhaps twenty times in all. Then I was almost word perfect in reading the Koran. . . . Some months afterwards my parents conferred with our relations about finishing off my study of the Koran and having me circumcised. . . . I was dressed in a fine raiment of gold and silver, and then brought before the company and ordered to recite whatever parts of the Koran people wished to hear, including my teacher. Many other learned men asked me questions on the reading of the Koran, concerning pronunciation and so forth. When I had answered, the *imam* or the *khatib* said a blessing and I was ordered to bow to my teacher, followed by my parents.

Next came the circumcision ceremony itself. With this, Abdullah attained the status of an adult Muslim man. He was then sent to a teacher to learn Tamil. There were many Tamil traders living in Malacca at the time, and the language was considered useful "for doing computations and accounts, and for purposes of conversation, because at that time Malacca was crowded with Indian merchants." He studies Tamil for two and a half years. Also around this time he is instructed by his father to go to the mosque every day and master the correct way to write the names of all the people who attend. He learns how to write Malay, copying the Koran and Malay manuscripts.

One day, a sea captain comes to the house to look for Abdullah's father, wanting to draw up a bond, being in debt to a Chinese merchant. The man waits and waits in vain for Abdullah's father to return home. Abdullah volunteers to write the bond himself, although "I had never in my life drawn up a bond like that before." But the captain, satisfied, signs the letter Abdullah has written and hands him money. Just then, Abdullah's father returns home. The captain shows Abdullah's father the bond, and Abdullah fears he is in for a scolding or worse. But his father simply smiles when he sees the bond. "You may use this letter, Captain. Take it to the house of your creditor." Then he reports smilingly to Abdullah's mother: "Now I have gained a child, just as if he were born to me this very day." And "from that day onwards, any written message, receipt, covenant, will, or the like which people brought to be written, my father ordered me to do so."

In this period, most people were illiterate. Being able to read and write Malay was an impressive skill, and people who could write beautiful letters using the adapted Arabic writing system known as Jawi were well respected as calligraphers. People who had this skill made a living as amanuenses, writing letters, drawing up business contracts and bonds, and copying documents. Abdullah followed in his father's footsteps and became a scribe.

From this point on, Abdullah continues to refine his studies of the Malay language. At the time, it was considered unusual for anyone to want to study Malay. Studying Arabic, the sacred language in which the Word of God was written, made sense, but Malay was different; such was the general idea at the time. Despite the prejudices of his time, Abdullah chose to study under experts in Malay, learning from them the "secrets of the Malay language." "I obtained all kinds of examples . . . I learnt a great many sayings, and fine combinations of words. From them I gleaned many of the artifices of Malay grammar; compound words and word combinations, the order of words, root words and derivatives, the force of words, euphony, affixations, associated words, the sense of words, their refinement, innuendos and specialized meanings."

This, then, was how Abdullah presented himself: as the descendant of an Arab from Yemen, of the family of Othman, whose name was Shaikh Abdul Kadir. He inherited his name from a man named Habib Abdullah, of the Haddad family. He was a good Muslim, a scribe, and someone who had acquired the "secrets of the Malay language." What is missing from this self-introduction?

One thing lacking is any mention of a state or nationality. When we introduce ourselves as "Japanese" or "Taiwanese" today, we take for granted the existence of the states of Japan and Taiwan (the Republic of China). But for Abdullah, the state was something that had nothing to do with his life or personal identity. For example, his story also contains the following passage:

> One day an instruction from the Secretary to the Government at Batavia was passed through Malacca Government to my father ordering him . . . to act as an emissary to the Malay chiefs, carrying a letter from Timmerman Thyssen.

The word used in Abdullah's original text (translated here as "chiefs") is "raja." These are the same figures that Raffles described in his letter as the "Malay kings." As we have seen, by the time Abdullah was writing his memoir in the mid-nineteenth century, the toddling leviathan that had been born in the Straits Settlements had already started to grow quite considerably. But Abdullah did not understand the state as an instrument of control like a modern state. In the Malay of his day, there were no words to describe a leviathan of this kind. As far as he was concerned, the Dutch and British governors and residents in Malacca and Singapore, together with the Malay kings in Riau, Palembang, and Pahang, were all equally "rajas," and although he might occasionally work in their service, the fact of their existence had nothing at all to do with his identity.

Another thing missing from Abdullah's self-description is any mention of the concept of race or ethnicity. It is interesting to compare his account with a description of him written by Thomson, the "white friend" (*orang putih*) mentioned at the beginning of Abdullah's own memoir:

In physiognomy he was a Tamilian of southern Hindustan: slightly bent forward, spare, energetic, bronze in complexion, oval-faced, high-nosed, one eye squinting outwards a little. He dressed in the usual style of Malacca Tamils. *Acheen se'luar*, check sarong, printed *baju*, square skull cap and sandals. He had the vigour and pride of the Arab, the perseverance and subtlety of the Hindoo—in language and national sympathy only was he a Malay.

The significance of this should be clear without any lengthy explanation. For Thomson, it was self-evident that the Tamils, Arabs, Hindus, and Malays each had their own distinctive ethnic or "racial" characteristics. It is this that makes him describe Abdullah with this combination of ethnic markers. It is precisely this kind of description that is missing from Abdullah's account.

But all of this was to change utterly in the space of a generation or two. Abdullah had three sons, who became government officials under Abu Bakar, the sultan of Johore, as the sultanate in the southern tip of the Malay Peninsula began to develop as a small leviathan during the second half of the nineteenth century under the supervision of the Straits Settlements.

His eldest son Hussein died in 1865, in an accident when there was an explosion onboard the *Johore*, the sultan's first steamship. His second son, Mohammad Khalid, established a "Malay School" in Johore. The third, Mohammad Ibrahim, rose to a position of some importance (an acting chancellor) in the local government. In other words, their fates were inextricably linked with the small leviathan state of Johore, which would be absorbed as a province (state) of British Malaya by the end of the nineteenth century. Because of this connection, his sons became "Malays."

What had changed?

Raffles' Plan for the Town of Singapore

It goes without saying that diverse groups of people have always existed in all places and at all times, differing in language, culture, religion, and customs, and with different habits of clothing, hairstyles, diet, and facial features. The question was how to deal with these various groups.

There was nothing new about this question. Systems of different kinds had been created in different places at different times. In the kingdom of Malacca, for example, foreigners were organized into groups according to their places of origin and allowed to govern their own affairs. This system was continued by the Portuguese and the Dutch. During the Dutch period, the population of Malacca was divided into Indians, Malays, Chinese, and Christians, each with a "*kapitan*" appointed as leader. But these groups were not racial or ethnic categories as we understand them today.

This is made clear by the fact that the three "ethnic" categories are juxtaposed with a fourth category: "Christians." An ethnic group is something one has no control over: if I am born as a "Japanese," I will remain in that ethnic category for the rest of my life. But anyone can choose to become a Christian. In fact, these "ethnic" or "racial" categories were juxtaposed with the religious category of "Christian" because they were much more fluid than they are today, and it was possible and indeed not unusual for someone to *become* "Indian," "Malay," or "Chinese" in the same way as one might choose to become a Christian. Hence the Batavian "Dutch" women in Lord Minto's letter: even someone of "native" blood, who understood only Malay and spoke no Dutch, who dressed in a sarong and *kebaya* and had a mouth stained red from chewing betel, felt comfortable calling herself "Dutch." At the time, "Dutch" was not a category that was defined in terms of race or nationality. It was merely a subcategory of the "Christian" group.

But these categories changed dramatically over the course of the nineteenth century. The drivers of leviathan, powerful British men like Lord Minto and Raffles, came to understand these categories in racial terms and made them fundamental to the way the administration was run. This is quite easy to see. Raffles said that although people differed "radically in customs, manners, religion, and language," and possessed "very different degrees of civilization," they could be referred to as Malays "for the sake of convenience." Whether these people thought of themselves as Malays or not was of little interest.

In the same way, Raffles and the other British administrators in the Straits Settlements classified people into ethnic categories for reasons of convenience. The administrators called people "Malays," "Indians," "Chinese," "Europeans," and so on, registered them according to these categories, organized them into separate residential areas, formulated different systems of civil law for them, and governed inheritance of property. This approach became fundamental to the administration of the Straits Settlements colonial government. A person might never have considered his or her identity in these terms. But once a person was classified as "Malay," he or she would be expected to live in the "Malay" district, be bound by "Malay" civic laws regarding marriage, divorce, and inheritance, and send his or her children to "Malay" schools. This identity as a "Malay," which originally had no great meaning, gradually came to assume a supreme importance, thanks to the power of leviathan. Over the course of the nineteenth century, this happened in the Straits Settlements (and British Malaya), the Dutch East Indies, and in other parts of Southeast Asia.

But how did this happen, in concrete terms? The perfect resource for helping us to understand what happened is the plan that Raffles drew up for the layout of the new settlement of Singapore. In 1819, the year Singapore was "founded," Raffles drew up a basic plan of how the new town should be laid out. He divided the people living in Singapore into various "communities." Each community would have its own designated residential area, and chiefs would be appointed and made responsible for maintaining order within the various "Asiatic" communities. This was the basic idea.

A group of seafaring Malays (*orang laut*, people of the sea) had lived on the banks of the Singapore River since before Raffles' arrival, under the leadership of their chief, or *temenggung*. Raffles decided to leave these "Malays" where they were. He designated the left bank of the river as the government district; this is where the Parliament, Supreme Court, and City Hall stand today. A military cantonment was to the north of this, with a church and "open plain." The "European" quarter was situated to the east of the cantonment, while the Chinese were allocated an area on the right bank of the Singapore River.

The plan was revised on the occasion of Raffles' last visit to Singapore, in 1823. A new commercial district was established on the right bank close to the mouth of the Singapore River, and the "Chinese" who had lived there were relocated further inland. There was a small hill in this area. A decision was made to level the hill and reclaim land from the swampy marshes along the shoreline. The area where the hill had stood became the central business district, where Raffles Place stands today. The marshes were turned into a wharf. Also at this time, the group of around 600 "Malays" who had previously lived along the Singapore River under their native chief or *temenggung* were moved to an area of the shoreline west of Chinatown, between Tanjong Pagar and Tanjong Braga. This meant that the river could now be used exclusively for commercial purposes, without the "Malay" population getting in the way.

On the left bank of the Singapore River, an "Arab" district was established to the east of the European town, together with a "Malay" *kampong* (or "village") under the leadership of the Riau sultan backed by Raffles, and a "Bugis" *kampong* farther to the east. Apart from the commercial district, the entire west bank of the river was set aside as a Chinese area, further divided into areas for Fujianese, Cantonese, Teochew, and so on. Another area further upriver was set aside for "Indians."

Based on Raffles' outline of the plan for the town, in 1828 Lieutenant Philip Jackson drew up what is known as the Jackson Plan. Everything is neatly set out according to Raffles' outline. The various residential districts are arranged in a neat grid, divided by straight roads that intersect at right angles. In the business district, the buildings are shown with tiled roofs and made of stone.

People were categorized as "Bugis," "Malays," or "Chinese" and assigned to separate living areas. These groups would only come together in the business district, where their respective offices, shops, and storehouses would nestle side-by-side. Under the authority of a single leviathan, these various communities, differing in terms of language, culture, religion, belief, and customs would coexist but not intermix, and except for meeting in the marketplace, would share no common social purpose: the British political economist J.S. Furnivall called this kind of society a "plural society." It was this kind of plural society that now started to develop in Singapore.

Of course, this was not a natural process. Once people had settled in a certain area, they were not easy to dislodge. Simply telling them,

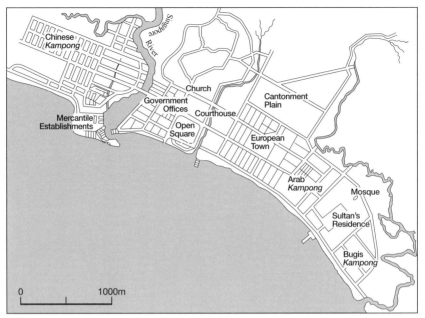

Plan of the town of Singapore, prepared by Lieutenant Jackson (1828)

"You belong to such-and-such a group; your place is over there," was not enough. When this happened, the Straits Settlements government prepared a piece of land and paid financial compensation. And if this didn't work, they would resort to force. In this way, the leviathan transformed precise racial categories into spatial reality within the town of Singapore according to Raffles' plan: Chinese, Malays, Arabs, Europeans, and Bugis. If Abdullah's "white friend" had told him, "You're a Malay," it's likely that Abdullah would have had no real sense of what this meant. Not that the word would have been entirely without meaning for him: for Abdullah, the "Malays" were the people who lived on the right bank of the Singapore River, to the far west of Chinatown, or to the far east of the "Arabs."

The Politics of Identity

To restate the facts so far, in more general terms: a map of society was drawn up based on racial categories, and the power of leviathan made this map into a social reality. As a result, what had begun as empty categories gradually took on a very real meaning. The departure point for this process was the census, by which leviathan counted and classified the people living under its control.

The first census of Singapore's population was carried out in 1824. Eleven thousand inhabitants were counted and divided into eight categories: Malays, Chinese, Bugis, Indians, Europeans, Arabs, Armenians, and others. This formed the basic pattern for subsequent censuses held in the Straits Settlements and British Malaya. During the nineteenth century, Malaya was a frontier zone that attracted a constant flow of new immigrants. It was not only the Chinese who were drawn here. They were joined by Japanese, Acehnese, Batak, Minangkabau, Javanese, Bugis, and other ethnic groups from Sumatra, Java, Celebes, and other parts of maritime Southeast Asia. And these people were all categorized in censuses, often in a highly arbitrary fashion.

In the nineteenth century, the Japanese were a subcategory of the Chinese. Similarly, the Acehnese, Bugis, and Javanese were all classed as types of "Malay." The "Malays" were regarded as the original inhabitants of Malaya, and according to this fiction, even newly arrived immigrants could be described as "sons of the soil." This continues to provide the rationale for the Malaysian government's *bumiputera* (native son) policies of positive discrimination to this day.

But that still lay far in the future, at this stage. More important for our discussion here is to remember that the administration of British Malaya was built on these foundations. Categories like "Malay," "Chinese," and "Indian" became fetishized, so that someone who was categorized as "Malay" came to think of himself as "Malay," even if in reality he might be the descendant of Shaikh Abdul Kadir, an Usman Arab from Yemen. In other words, the categories of ethnicity and race came about as the result of censuses and the power of leviathan, and eventually such categories were internalized and taken for granted.

Naturally this does not apply only to Singapore and Malaysia. Race/ethnicity became a meaningful category in the same way all across Southeast Asia: in British Malaya, the Dutch East Indies, the Spanish-ruled

Philippines, and eventually also in Siam (Thailand) under the Chakri dynasty. And everywhere, this gave birth to a new kind of politics.

First came the politics of numbers. The inhabitants were counted and categorized according to ethnicity and region (administrative units), income level, educational background, age, and so on. This revealed clear majority and minority groups. (For example, population statistics revealed for the first time that in the Dutch East Indies the "Chinese" made up a mere three percent of the total population.) Statistics on income, education, and labor were also grouped by ethnicity, revealing any disparities that existed between ethnic groups in terms of income, education, and employment. It was this that led to the discovery of the "overseas Chinese problem."

Second, the mestizo or mixed-race population disappeared. Of course, they did not *literally* disappear. Rather, it was the category that vanished. And this led to the politics of identity. In population statistics, ethnic categories have a fictional quality that makes them monolithic and indivisible. Assume for the sake of illustration that the population of Malaysia consisted solely of "Malays" and "Chinese." Everyone in the population would have to belong to one category or the other. But the reality is much more complex than this. Even in the case of a mixed-race person of Malay and Chinese descent, as Benedict Anderson reminds us, many different combinations inevitably exist: "half-Malay, half-Chinese," "one-quarter Malay, three-quarters Chinese," "one-eighth Malay, seven-eighths Chinese," and so on. But complex categories like this are unthinkable in a census. Everyone gets categorized arbitrarily into either the Malay or the Chinese group. In this situation, there is no place for the mestizos. What happens, then? The only choice is for the mestizo population to assimilate into one of the other categories: Europeans, Chinese, Malays, and so on.

And so the betel-chewing "Dutch" woman who couldn't speak Dutch ensured that her children received a Dutch education, and by the end of the nineteenth century the Eurasians in the Indies had become quite similar to middle-class Dutch people in the Netherlands. Around the same time, the mestizos in the Philippines became transformed into "Filipinos." Groups such as the Babas of Malacca and the Peranakan of Java, who were the descendants of the "respectable" Chinese who controlled opium revenue farming under the British and Dutch, came to be regarded as retrograde "Chinese" who spoke only Malay. They were often attacked as "un-Chinese" by their Chinese "countrymen."

It became the rule that all "Dutch" people should behave in a fittingly "Dutch" manner, while the Chinese and Malays likewise had to conform to the norms and expectations made of them by society. This change transformed the societies of Southeast Asia between the end of the nineteenth and the beginning of the twentieth centuries.

CHAPTER FIVE

The Logic of
the Civilizing Project

Awhole genre of Dutch literature is devoted to works set in the Indies. One of the classics of the genre is *De Stille Kracht* (translated into English as *The Hidden Force*), by Louis Couperus, which contains the following passage:

> The carriage had left the wealthier part of the town and entered the Chinese quarter . . . When the carriage approached, they [the Chinese] rose and remained standing respectfully. The Javanese for the most part—those who were well brought up and knew their manners—squatted. . . . when the carriage drove into the Arab quarter—a district of ordinary houses, but gloomy, lacking in style, with life and prosperity hidden away behind closed doors; with chairs in the verandah, but the master of the house gloomily sitting cross-legged on the floor, following the carriage with a black look—this quarter seemed even more mysterious than the fashionable part of Labuwangi and seemed to radiate its unutterable mystery like an atmosphere of Islam that spread over the whole town, as though it were Islam that had poured forth the dusty, fatal melancholy of resignation which filled the shuddering, noiseless evening.

Couperus wrote his novel in Dutch for a Dutch audience at the end of the nineteenth century, when he was living in the provincial town of Pasuruan in East Java. The passage I have just quoted describes the events on a cloudless evening in a fictional provincial capital presumably modeled on Pasuruan. The passage describes the scenery seen from the carriage windows as the Dutch resident and his family ride through the district of Labuwangi. The carriage enters the Chinese quarter. "We" (the novel's Dutch readers) are invited by Couperus to look out from the carriage with them and share in the view of the scenery that surrounds them. Bustling crowds of people hurriedly make way. The queue-wearing Chinese snap to attention; the Javanese squat low on one knee. Everything is as it ought to be, and there is apparently nothing to threaten the peace and order of the scene. And then the carriage enters the Arab quarter, lined with rows of whitewashed houses. Our eyes are drawn to a man squatting on the floor, looking out at "us" with a dark, brooding look on his face. We look back at him. Probably an Arab. But the more we look at him, the more mysterious he becomes. Once we notice this hint of mystery, the order is no longer as stable as it seemed just moments ago. Mystery fills the evening air of Labuwangi, and we begin to see mystery everywhere we look: in the Chinese standing to attention, the respectful Javanese, the Arab crouching in his doorway, the *haji* with his white turban, the Javanese nobles with their masklike faces.

The scene that Couperus depicts here is fictional. But it captures very well the isolation and outsider status of the Dutch in the East Indies at the end of the nineteenth century. In the plural society of the East Indies, with white Europeans at its summit, the Dutch were both present but apart, constantly beset by the feeling that they were on stage and being observed. And once "we" realize that we are being looked at, everything we see in return—the Chinese, the natives, the Arabs—starts to appear strange and full of foreboding, even when there is nothing obviously wrong. There is something here we do not understand, something that is hidden from our sight. This sense of something mysterious and unknowable gradually changes the civic order of white society in the East Indies—in the same way that a piano brought out from the Netherlands will eventually lose pitch in this alien climate, no matter how many times it is tuned.

There is a new sense of order here. In the nineteenth century, order was something that could be seen. Remember Raffles' plan for the town of Singapore. "Europeans" (whites), "Chinese," "Arabs," and "natives" were each allocated their own residential quarters and required by law to wear distinctive dress and hairstyles. What the Chinese and natives were looking at, what they were thinking—these were not things that anyone cared to know about. "We" were the ones in control, and that was all that mattered. But by the time Couperus was writing, order could no longer be accepted in these terms. It had become more internalized. And this transformation gave rise to a new kind of liberal project: to strip the mystery and "unknowability" from things the colonizers saw and could not understand. It was no longer enough for the Chinese to follow form by standing to attention or for the Javanese to squat respectfully. They must be made to behave in their hearts. This was the basic thrust of the project, which was carried out in the name of "civilizing" the natives. How was this project carried out, and what changes did it bring? And why was a new liberal project felt to be necessary at this period between the end of the nineteenth century and the beginning of the twentieth?

The Birth of the Colonial World

Over the last two chapters, we have looked at how leviathan-like states were born and plural societies formed in Southeast Asia over the course of the nineteenth century. This process was mostly complete by the latter part of the nineteenth century—the period between the 1870s and 1890s. By this time, a colonial world in the strict sense of the term had come into being.

What kind of world was it?

A comparison of two maps is a good way to understand what had happened. (See page 90.) The first map illustrates Southeast Asia in the age of "mandala states" at the end of the eighteenth century. Apart from the small states formed around Manila in the Spanish-ruled Philippines and Batavia in the Dutch East Indies, leviathan states have not even been born. The second map shows Southeast Asia at the end of the nineteenth century. By this time, the leviathans have achieved substantial growth and divide the whole of Southeast Asia among themselves. Borderlines now show these divisions on a map; once we enter the twentieth century, these borderlines will increasingly come to define the states and their societies.

This was the most important change that took place in Southeast Asia in the second half of the nineteenth century. Within these territories demarcated by borders, states gradually extended their power from the center to the peripheries. The characteristics of these leviathans and the circumstances of their growth differed from country to country. Nevertheless, by the second half of the nineteenth century, populations everywhere had been disarmed and a "colonial peace" had been achieved. The state embarked on major construction projects: constructing port facilities, laying telegraph and telephone cables, building roads and railways, and so on. Colonial capitalism grew on these foundations: tin mines and rubber plantations in Malaya, tobacco plantations around Medan in eastern Sumatra, sugar plantations in East Java and in Negros, in the Philippines. Throughout Southeast Asia, this led to the development of an economy built around the export of primary produce. As this economy expanded, it provided the financial support for the further growth of the leviathans.

Another major change that took place in Southeast Asia in the second half of the nineteenth century was the formation of plural societies and the growth of white European communities within them. We have already seen how plural societies came into existence: societies in which groups of people differing in language, culture, religion, beliefs, and customs lived under the authority of the same leviathan state, coexisting but never intermixing and seldom meeting except in the marketplace, and with no common social purpose. In Southeast Asia, these plural societies were everywhere organized according to a racial hierarchy, with white Europeans at the top and "natives" at the bottom. In between were the Chinese, Arabs, Indians, and other "foreign Asiatics." (The Japanese belonged to this category in the nineteenth century but were promoted to become "honorary whites" in the twentieth century.)

During the second half of the nineteenth century, larger communities of "white" Europeans grew within these plural societies, particularly after the opening of the Suez Canal in 1869. Previously, European men had come to Southeast Asia alone, but beginning in the mid-nineteenth century, white women began to arrive as well, establishing British and Dutch middle-class family lives for themselves in cities like Penang, Singapore, and Batavia, as well as on plantations in places like the east coast of Sumatra and Johore. But they were surrounded at all times by Javanese and Chinese amahs, maidservants, and houseboys, as well as Malay peasants, Chinese merchants, and Arab moneylenders. They did not understand the natives'

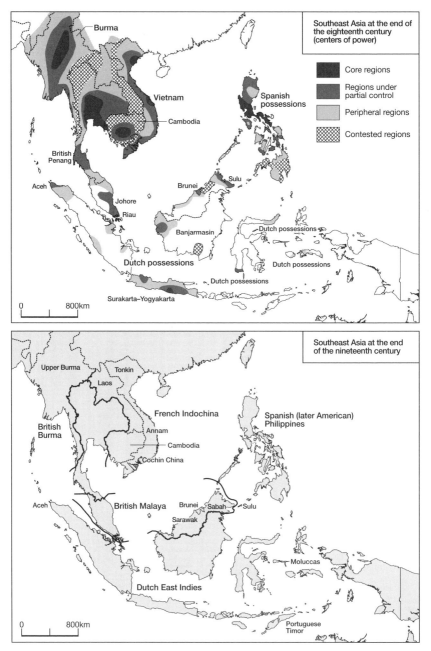

Two maps showing how leviathan states not yet born at the end of the eighteenth century encompassed the entire region by the end of the nineteenth

languages well enough. Simply having these strange, unknowable people around them made them uneasy—and they tended to react hysterically when plantation workers showed signs of restlessness or when there was a break-in or burglary. Maintaining order was now the biggest task facing the colonial governments, and the leviathan states had to work to ensure the safety and welfare of these white communities above all else.

Another major change that took place in Southeast Asia in the latter half of the nineteenth century was that the leviathans themselves changed in nature as they developed and grew. By the end of the nineteenth century, the leviathan states that had started their toddling progress in the 1820s and 1830s had not merely divided the whole of Southeast Asia among themselves but had brought the colonial societies under their direct supervision and control. Triangulation and censuses were used to draw up cadastral ledgers and registers of citizens. In the Straits Settlements, British officials who could speak Chinese (Hokkien, Cantonese, Teochew, etc.) began registration of the Chinese secret societies, while in the Dutch East Indies, Dutch bureaucrats who had studied Javanese and "local" languages such as Minangkabau carried out surveys of customs and traditional laws.

This brought a shift from indirect to direct rule. In Java under the forced cultivation system in the mid-nineteenth century, for example, the feudal landowners who had been in place since the time of the Mataram Sultanate still occupied strategic positions in the East Indies state as regents (*bupati*). The state placed the Javanese nobility in charge of the indigenous bureaucracy and used them as intermediaries between the Dutch and indigenous departments within the machinery of state. But that was not all. Throughout the nineteenth century, the state headed by the Dutch bureaucrats was connected via the native bureaucracy and the Chinese networks to the twilight zone between the legal and illegal worlds, peopled by Javanese and Chinese itinerant merchants, local toughs, gamblers, and prostitutes. The Javanese nobility controlled the informal networks that led down into this twilight zone and when it suited their purposes could use these toughs and gamblers to exert real control over the rural regions of Java. This was what underwrote their power. The Dutch were probably hardly aware of these networks at first—or, if they were, they could do nothing about them. But by the end of the century these networks had become visible to the Dutch as well. The arbitrary "tyranny" of the *bupati* became a topic of frequent criticism, and these informal networks of power came under Dutch attack.

The same can be said of opium farming. The system of opium farming made a massive contribution to the growth of the leviathan states. But by the end of the nineteenth century, the same system had come to be regarded as a dangerous source of funding for the Chinese secret societies that exploited Javanese farmers and Chinese coolies. A government monopoly was introduced and the "respectable" Chinese who had earned the trust of the British and Dutch lost their power. But this did not mean that the Chinese networks simply disappeared. The secret societies were attacked as "a state within a state," and one after another their leaders were expelled from the country.

In both cases the logic was the same. Here was something premodern, opaque, and corrupt that needed to be "reformed." In the Dutch East Indies, in the name of an "Ethical Policy" supposedly for the development and progress of native society, the government implemented adminstrative reform and enhanced educational opportunities for the indigenous elite, while in the Straits Settlements a Chinese Protectorate was established "for the protection of the Chinese population," and steps were taken to suppress the secret societies and register immigrants into the colony.

Looked at in this way, we can see that a new world was being formed in Southeast Asia at the end of the nineteenth and the beginning of the twentieth centuries. In the second half of the nineteenth century, Japan was in the process of modernizing itself, promoting industrialization, advancing education, and putting together a modern state equipped with a modern army and navy, under the *fukoku kyōhei* (enrich the country, strengthen the army) policy. A similar process of modernization had taken place in Southeast Asia, based on colonial capitalism and colonial states. By the 1910s, this led to the development of major cities like Manila, Singapore, and Batavia, which struck Japanese travelers at the time as being much more "modern" than Japan. The chief question for the "civilizing" project was how to create a stable order in this new world.

The "Civilizing" Project

The project was founded on an extremely simple idea. If "we" could not know what the Arab with the gloomy face was looking at, we should change things so that we did know. And if we could not know what the Javanese, with their masklike faces, were thinking, then we should change things so that they thought like us. The light of Western civilization should be used to illuminate and enlighten the darkness of Asia—that was the essence of the project.

This project was attempted most systematically in the Dutch East Indies at the beginning of the twentieth century. The key to the success of the project was understood to be educating the native elite in Dutch. To understand why, it is enough to look at *Through Darkness into Light* (*Door Duisternis tot Licht*), a collection of letters by a young Javanese woman named Kartini, who was embraced by Dutch liberals as representing the "modern awakening" of the Javanese.

Kartini was a contemporary of Louis Couperus. She was born in 1879 in the provincial town of Jepara, on the north coast of Java, where her father was a nobleman who served as a high-ranking native official in the local government. She was one of the first Javanese women to receive an education in Dutch at the school for Europeans. She wrote in Dutch magazines about the self-awareness of the Javanese and the need for education for girls, and carried on a correspondence with numerous Dutch people until her premature death in 1904 at the age of 25. After her death a selection of this correspondence was published by one of her friends, J. H. Abendanon, a liberal who had served as director of education in the government of the Dutch East Indies. In his book *Karutini no fūkei* [Kartini's Image of Java's Landscape], the Japanese scholar Tsuchiya Kenji wrote along the following lines about Kartini's writing as seen in her published correspondence.

In the Javanese *wayang* (shadow puppet theater), for example, it would be meaningless to understand what the narrator says about nature as a simple description of nature itself. Nature is entirely integrated with human affairs. It is depicted in a way that hints at destiny in the human world or as a symbol to praise the powerful of this world (classically, the power of the king). This means that descriptions of nature consist of traditional set phrases and tropes. In Kartini, however, nature is depicted as itself, like a landscape in a painting. At the core of her writing was the self: an "I" who saw and heard and wrote of her own experiences. It was thanks to this sense of self, which she obtained from the Dutch "I," that Kartini could describe nature in the same way that a painter depicts it on canvas.

This is a penetrating observation. We can perhaps add to it as follows. By acquiring the Dutch "I," Kartini learned to depict what she saw like an artist painting on canvas and became able to objectify what she saw. This meant she could render the world she saw visible to her Dutch readers. It became possible for the Dutch to see what her "I" was looking at. The "mystery" of which Couperus wrote was mysterious no longer. This is why Dutch liberals were so eager to welcome Kartini as emblematic of the modern awakening of the "natives." She was unmistakable proof of the success of the civilizing project.

The Birth of Modern Politics

But the significance of Kartini's acquisition of the Dutch "I" did not stop there. For Kartini, this acquired ability to see the world in objective terms came as a huge shock. She speaks of this shock in her letters as follows: one day, not long before she is ready to graduate from her elementary school, a Dutch classmate asks her what she wants to be when she grows up. She doesn't know what to reply, and when she gets home, she asks her father. Her father says nothing but merely smiles and pinches her cheek. What she is saying here is quite clear, I believe. At this moment, she discovers that it is possible to imagine an "I" that is different from the "I" that exists here and now as a social reality. And this comes as a great shock.

While this shock remained something written of in Dutch by bilingual "natives" like Kartini who had received an education in Dutch, it was merely something personal. The number of bilingual "natives" was quite limited, after all. But once the Dutch "I" was translated into Malay (today's Indonesian), this discovery took on a major political significance. I am not saying anything particularly difficult or profound here. If I do not know anything but the "I" that exists as a social reality in the here and now, I have no choice but to accept that reality as something permanent and unshakable. But if a large number of people can suddenly imagine a different "I" for themselves than the one that exists in the here and now as a social reality, it is only a matter of time before they start to ask themselves: "What if I were Dutch?" "What if I were the governor-general of the Dutch East Indies?" "What if I were a regent?" Once this happens, the colonial and social order of the Dutch East Indies can no longer be accepted as self-evident.

It was this discovery that gave birth to modern politics—or, to put it more plainly, gave rise to the kind of thing we would immediately recognize as politics today. For example, if we see dozens of people holding placards in front of the U.S. Embassy in Jakarta, we immediately understand that we are looking at a demonstration. Or if hundreds of students are gathered on the campus of the University of Indonesia and someone in front of them is speaking into a microphone, we immediately recognize that what we are seeing is a rally or assembly of some kind. This was the kind of politics that now started in these colonial societies. Rallies were held, newspapers published, political parties formed, and strikes organized. All these developments took place around the 1910s. Today, this is generally understood as the birth of nationalism: because it was from within this new type of modern politics that independence movements were born—movements, that is to say, that sought to "reclaim" the leviathan state, that had been transplanted into Southeast Asia from above and from outside as an alien species, as something that was "our own," and to "restore" it to the people. But the new politics also released something else, something that can only be described as the energy of chaos.

A good way to understand what this meant is to look at what happened in Indonesia, for example, in the 1910s and 1920s. A bilingual Javanese called Soewardi Soerjaningrat wrote an essay called "If I were a Dutchman" ("Als ik eens Nederlander was"). This was translated into Malay in 1912, earning its author a sentence of exile to the Netherlands. The same year, the first mass rally was held in the East Indies, heralding the arrival of modern politics in that part of the world. In 1916 and 1917, numerous labor unions and farmers' unions were formed and strikes took place across the country. In 1920, the Communist Union of the Indies (Perserikatan

Komunis di Hindia) was formed, the first communist party in Asia, changing its name to the Communist Party of Indonesia (Partai Komunis Indonesia, or PKI) in 1925. Under the leadership of the party, and in the name of "revolution," armed uprisings took place in Java and Sumatra beginning in 1926 and continuing into 1927.

Why did this happen? I think there were two main reasons. The first is quite simple. The new modern politics began when a large number of "natives" could imagine for the first time a different "I" from the one that existed in the here and now as a social reality. While people like these were asking themselves, "What if I were a Dutchman?" or "What if I were the governor-general of the Dutch East Indies?" then what was at stake was the colonial order of the Dutch East Indies. But once they started to ask, "What if I were district chief?" or "What if I were a sultan?" then it was the social order of society itself that became the issue. It is not surprising that some people found ideas like "revolution" and "constructing a new society" persuasive at this time.

The other, more important, reason lay in language itself. It seems fair to say that the word "I" in Malay was not yet domesticated like the Dutch word "I." It was a wild and untamed "I." To see this a little better, we can compare the words for "I" in the two languages. By acquiring the Dutch "I," Kartini became the very image of the ideal "native" in whom Dutch liberals could pin their hopes. This was not merely because it allowed the Dutch to "read" what Kartini was seeing and thinking. By studying Dutch, Kartini imbibed the social map and authority inherent in the Dutch language. Look, for example, at the way in which she describes a local beach near Jepara that she called "Klein Scheveningen":

When we enjoy a concert of birdsong or sweet music, in which we quite lose ourselves, how thankful we are that God has not created us deaf! Or when we are at Klein Scheveningen, that idyllic spot by the sea, where everything breathes quiet and peace and poetry, and see the sun go down so beautifully, then we cannot be grateful enough that we have good eyes to enjoy it. And in the delighted gaze, which in quiet enjoyment follows the wonderful light that plays in colors upon the rippling water, and in the heavens above, there is consecrated a quiet prayer of thanksgiving to the invisible Great Spirit who created and governs everything!

Probably no lengthy explanation is required here. Here, Kartini's "I" is tied up inseparably with the social map inherent in the Dutch language: through the "concert of birdsong" (not the traditional Javanese gamelan or the popular Batavian *krontjong* songs such as "Bengawan Solo," but a concert such as "we Dutch" might attend at the Concertgebouw in Amsterdam), through her local "Klein Scheveningen," and through the "invisible Great Spirit." (The original Scheveningen is a beach close to The Hague; in terms of its size and beauty, it would perhaps be fairer to describe the Dutch version as "*klein*.")

But as soon as this Dutch "I" was replaced by its Malay equivalent, the "I" suddenly started to move in a wild, untamed region in which there were no maps worthy of the name. This was particularly true of Malay. Malay was a lingua franca, and therefore a language that belonged to no one in particular—and that could become anyone's language. It did not yet contain a stable social map of society and did not contain the authority inherent in a language like Dutch. In a language of this kind, the "I" was not tethered but drifted at random.

But this "drifting" was not a phenomenon that was limited to Malay. It happened elsewhere, and for a simple reason. As U Nu, Burma's first prime minister said, the modern state is like a car. And just as a car has no ontological raison d'être, neither does the state itself have any inherent reason for existing. States of this kind were transplanted into various parts of Southeast Asia and by the end of the nineteenth century had come to control society with their overwhelming power. But what were they? What meaning did this new situation have? The languages of Southeast Asia, which had previously supported the mandala states, did not have an answer to these questions. The authority of language was shattered. The drifting of the "I" served to indicate this absence of authority.

Leviathan's Twentieth-Century Turning Point

The question for the colonial governments was how to respond to this crisis. The only prescription offering a fundamental resolution to the problem was nationalism: to say "this state belongs to us, the people," and give the leviathan an ontological reason for existing. But this was something that colonial governments could not do. What did they do instead?

In the Dutch East Indies, the government took two main steps. One was to bulk up leviathan, in particular by modernizing the policing apparatus. A modern police force was organized in the 1910s, and in 1919 this was augmented by the addition of a political police unit. Also, in the 1920s, in response to the activities of the Communist International (Comintern), an international system came into being to enable cooperation between political police forces in the various colonies of Southeast Asia.

The other was to organize a "prison archipelago" and create a Malay map of the society of the East Indies. This requires some explanation. As I have mentioned, an armed uprising took place in the East Indies in 1926–27 with the aim of bringing about a revolution under the leadership of the Communist Party of Indonesia. This was promptly suppressed. But the event itself came as a huge shock to the government and to white society. Immediately after the uprising, the government decided on mass arrest and incarceration of communist activists, and in 1927 a prison camp was constructed at Tanah Merah (Red Earth), upstream on the Digul River in Dutch New Guinea. By the end of the 1920s, some 1,300 political criminals and their families had been incarcerated there. Although some were released for "good behavior," from this date on Digul became a major center of incarceration. The communists were not the only ones to be sent here; republican and nationalist leaders and activists from other "revolutionary" parties were also imprisoned here. By the end of the 1920s, Digul had become synonymous with "prison." In the code used by the communist underground, prison was referred to as "hospital," and "Digul" was the "central hospital." The entire East Indies came to be imagined as a prison archipelago.

It was in this way that the government of the East Indies put together a Malay map of society. If people when they hear words like "Moscow," "Comintern," "Republic of Indonesia Party," "Communist Party," "revolution," "independence," and the like automatically associate these terms with ideas like "police," "political police," "arrest," "jail," "exile," and "Digul," these terms come to be marked with a "No Trespass" sign in people's minds. If some people still join the "Communist Party" and call for "independence" and "revolution," it is sufficient to demonstrate the reality of the fate that awaits them: police, arrest, jail, and Digul. This could be seen in a sense as aspects of the term "policing." We tend to think of policing as maintaining law and order and clamping down on crime, but in fact the word has a broader meaning. And the ideal form of policing is self-policing.

To create a situation in which there is a policeman inside every citizen, so that people control, regulate, and observe themselves—this is the ideal. So that whenever one is tempted to do something wrong, the policeman inside him/her shouts out a warning and tells him/her to stop. By turning the East Indies into a prison archipelago and creating a map of society in Malay, with stark "No Trespass" signs in front of words like "Moscow" and "Communist Party," the government was trying to impress self-policing on the native population. The civilizing project eventually turned into a police state.

When we look at things in this way, it becomes clear that a certain kind of logic was always attached to the idea of "looking" in the civilizing project. "We" were being looked at: once we notice this, "we" look at "them" but find that the more we look, the more mysterious they become. What are they thinking, what are they looking at? If we do not know the answers to these questions, we must change things so that we do. This is the moment at which the civilizing project begins. "We" must teach them our "I": that was the fundamental strategy. But this created a new problem. Modern politics was born, exposing the absence of authority in native languages. It was no longer enough simply to supervise them and ensure that they did not think inappropriate thoughts. The ideal of policing is self-policing. We must remind them that we are watching them at all times and make sure that they start to watch over themselves. And when this happened, the logical consequence of the civilizing project was a police state.

What was the significance of the civilizing project in world history? I am reminded in this context of another liberal project that began around the same time: the project of "Americanization" that sought to turn diverse immigrants differing in terms of language, religion, ethnicity, and origin into American citizens. In his paper on Americanism, Furuya Jun writes along the following lines about "Fordism" as a model of twentieth-century Americanization.

Henry Ford once remarked: "I am more a manufacturer of men than of automobiles." True to his word, his approach to managing his workers sought to mold them into ideal Americans, by dealing with the totality of his workers' lives: not just in the factory but in their home lives and in their neighborhoods. One of the controlling principles in Ford's factories was the idea of "interchangeable parts." This principle applied not only to automobile parts but to workers as well. The ideal was a world in which the personal norms and practices of workers stemming from ethnicity and traditional customs had been totally eradicated, a world in which people would function like interchangeable parts of a machine. Ford's project was built on the model of a new type of person, a worker who possessed the middle-class values of reason and self-control and was adaptable to mechanization, one who would produce steady and reliable results from his place in the chain and thus contribute to industrial society as a whole. By following this model, he sought to create a new type of person: a kind of human engineering. What was revolutionary about this plan was that it did not seek to isolate workers in space, as the company town utopias of the nineteenth century had done, but to change them from the inside by providing incentives in many aspects of their lives both as productive workers and active consumers, thus freeing individuals and groups from the ties of history.

Thinking like this produced twentieth-century Americanism. This project is still with us today, because Americanization is the driving power behind American industrial capitalism itself. By contrast, the civilizing project failed and went bankrupt long ago, despite the continued existence of a few believers like John Howard, the Australian prime minister who intervened in the East Timor crisis in the name of "civilization." Today the project is totally anachronistic. The reason is simple. Just like Raffles' liberalism project, the civilizing project was one that relied on leviathan as its agent. Industrial capitalism, of the kind that provided the driving power for Americanization, didn't yet exist in Southeast Asia. Consequently, the project was already bankrupt by the time leviathan was transformed into a police state. This was shown quite clearly during the Japanese invasions of Southeast Asia. Apart from the Philippines, the "natives" of Southeast Asian countries hardly resisted the Japanese armies and merely looked on as their white "masters" surrendered and fled, as if it had nothing to do with them. During the Japanese occupation and the period of revolution and counterrevolution that followed, the leviathan states collapsed like a house of cards. For all practical purposes, the British-led regional order begun in the age of Raffles also came to an end at this time.

CHAPTER SIX

The New Imperial Order

The 1940s were a time of war, revolution and counterrevolution, during which major tectonic shifts took place in the political and economic structure of the world. During this time, the regional order in "East Asia" changed dramatically from the order that had prevailed since the nineteenth century. To understand how significant this change was, it is enough to consider briefly the map when we think of "East Asia" today.

On the continent is the People's Republic of China. On the Korean Peninsula, North and South Korea face each other in uneasy truce, while the Republic of China (Taiwan) and the PRC glare at each other across the Taiwan Strait. Behind them lies Japan; to the south, Vietnam, the Philippines, Indonesia, and the other countries of Southeast Asia. This new map came into being at the end of the 1940s. It was brought about by significant changes, including the arrival of the United States as a superpower, the dismantling of the Japanese empire, the founding of the People's Republic of China, and the independence of the various Southeast Asian countries. What kind of political and economic order was formed in Asia after the tectonic shifts of the 1940s?

A New Regional Order

The most important role in the formation of a new regional order in Asia was played by the United States—which is not to say that the United States was able to shape a new order as it pleased. Nevertheless, when we look at the order that was constructed in the region after the upheavals of the 1940s finally subsided, there can be no doubt that the foundational ideas that informed the order came from Washington, where they were hatched by people like Dean Acheson, George F. Kennan, and John Foster Dulles.

At the time, the American government had the power, money, and will to put these ideas into practice.

From Washington's point of view, there were two major problems in Asia in 1949–50. One was how to deal with the threat of international communism, and how to contain the Soviet Union and the People's Republic of China. The second concerned Japan: how could the United States rebuild Japan economically and make it independent as an American ally, while ensuring that it never again became a threat to the United States?

Japan was the key to resolving both these problems. Japan was to become the strategic center for the construction of an informal American empire in Asia, just as Singapore, Hong Kong, and Shanghai had been for Britain as it put together its free trade empire in the mid-nineteenth century. This was only natural. What the United States needed in the region was a "workshop" and a "military logistics base." And Japan was the only place that could fulfil these conditions. This fact was sufficient to guarantee Japan a position of central importance in Asia. But this position had to be based on the proviso that Japan did not threaten the structural superiority of the United States within the Asian regional order. How to construct a system along these lines: this was the fundamental question that the United States faced.

The answer the United States reached in national security terms is well known: the so-called "double containment" strategy. Under this system, international communism would be contained by a line passing from Japan through Southeast Asia and India to the oil-producing regions of the Persian Gulf, along what Acheson referred to as a "great crescent." This was the first strand of the containment strategy. Like the spokes of a wheel, a security system was built around a series of bilateral security treaties and military basing agreements signed between the United States and Japan, South Korea, Taiwan, the Philippines, Thailand, and other countries, with the United States as the hub. These agreements guaranteed forward deployment of forces under the U.S. Pacific Command in Hawaii.

The second strand involved the containment of Japan. This perhaps requires a little explanation. By the end of the 1940s, it was only a matter of time before Japan regained political independence. But the United States did not want Japan to become a threat again after it became independent and rebuilt its economy. How could the United States ensure that this did not happen? The answer provided by George Kennan, U.S. director of policy planning at the time, was that the United States should maintain a light hold on Japan's jugular, so that it could knock Japan out whenever it became necessary to do so simply by applying more pressure. The way to achieve this was to integrate Japan's military into the U.S.-led security system in Asia and ensure that the United States controlled Japan's energy supply.

Japan thus became the cornerstone of the U.S.-led regional security system in Asia. Japan's military strength was incorporated into the U.S.-led security system, and Japan itself became (like Germany in Europe) a "semi-sovereign" state: this was the basic condition and proviso of the U.S.-Japan Alliance.

In the economic sphere, the answer was to construct a system of triangular trade between Japan, Southeast Asia, and the United States. U.S. Secretary of State John Foster Dulles, for instance, urged Japanese Prime Minister Yoshida Shigeru to regard reparations to Asian countries as an investment in the future and said that Japan should look to conclude negotiations over reparations and restore diplomatic relations with Southeast Asian countries as quickly as possible, as a step toward economic cooperation. The thinking behind this was quite simple and straight-forward. To rebuild its economy, Japan needed to import raw materials and secure an export market for its manufactured products. Before the war, China had fulfilled both these conditions. But since the dismantling of the Japanese empire and the founding of the People's Republic of China, this economic relationship had collapsed. In addition, at a time when the United States was seeking to "contain" China, it would not be in the American interest for Japan to become dependent on China again for its import and export markets. What should be done instead? Southeast Asia would take China's place, exporting raw materials to Japan and importing its manufactured products. This would achieve two aims at once, helping Japan's economic recovery while promoting economic development in Southeast Asia. The United States would provide the dollars necessary to ensure that this system ran smoothly and thus develop a triangular trade relationship linking Japan, Southeast Asia, and the United States. This was the thinking behind the idea. Southeast Asia now came to have a real significance for Japan for the first time; Japan's relationship with Southeast Asia started as part of the construction of the triangular trade system between Japan, Southeast Asia, and the United States. As a natural consequence, the relationship was primarily based on economic cooperation.

This was the basic idea. Of course, there is always a gap between ideals and reality. The political and economic order in Asia was not immediately built in accordance with the schemes of the United States. A simple review of history will suffice to make this clear. The decisive factor in Japan's postwar recovery was the surge in demand created by the Korean War and the U.S. market. During the 1950s, problems over reparations and other issues meant that Japan's "return" to Southeast Asia was frustratingly slow, and efforts were even made to explore the possibilities for economic cooperation with South Asia instead. It was only in the latter half of the 1960s that economic cooperation between Japan and Southeast Asia got on track. Nor was a regional political order achieved exactly in line with American ideas. In the 1960s, Sukarno challenged the United States by calling for a Pyongyang-Peking-Jakarta axis; in the 1970s, Communist victories in Indochina forced the United States to withdraw from mainland Southeast Asia. Nevertheless, by the end of the 1960s, a reasonably stable new political and economic order had come into being in the maritime parts of the region, stretching from South Korea and Japan through Taiwan and Hong Kong to the Philippines, Thailand, Malaysia, Singapore, and Indonesia. This order was built on the foundations of the U.S.-led security system and the triangular trade system between the United States, Southeast Asia (as well as South Korea and Taiwan), and Japan. This structure continues to form the basis for the regional order in East Asia today. Eventually, in other words, the scheme devised by people like Acheson, Kennan, and Dulles in Washington in 1949–50 was achieved, despite some gaps in the details. This is something that should surprise us. How was it possible?

This is a complex question. In simple terms, the following is probably a fair enough account. The regional order that the United States constructed in Asia after World War II was one that, unlike the previous colonial empires, did not require territorial control. It was an informal empire that did not contradict or go against the formal system of sovereign states. The problem was how to contain challenges to this order, and how to integrate into it the countries of the region. The United States achieved this through two main means: semi-sovereignty and hegemony.

I have already talked about semi-sovereignty: this involved what Kennan described as a light hold on the Japanese jugular. I use the term here to designate states that cannot truly be described as sovereign states

U.S. diplomat George Kennan
(Photo: AP/Aflo)

according to the nineteenth-century European ideal type that Max Weber presumably had in mind when he defined the state. After World War II, the former colonial empires disappeared, and a huge number of new states came to cover the globe—incomparably more than had existed before the war. But most of these could hardly be described as truly sovereign when judged by the ideal type of nineteenth-century European states. In East Asia, the only country that could be described as a fully sovereign state in the classical sense today is China. In the other countries—including Japan, South Korea, and many of the countries of Southeast Asia—U.S. power is "built in" to the machinery of state in one way or another.

It is worth adding here that this concept of "semi-sovereignty" can help us understand the anomalous position China occupies within the Asian regional order. China entered the East Asian regional economic order toward the end of the 1970s, following normalization of diplomatic relations with the United States and Japan over the course of the decade. But China is not a part of the U.S.-led regional security system. It continues to play a nineteenth-century-style sovereign state game; for example, by refusing to rule out the use of force to resolve the Taiwan issue. In principle, only the United States is allowed to play this kind of game within the Asian regional order. This is the essence of Pax Americana. But China does not accept this. In other words, China occupies an ambiguous position: it is half inside the regional order and half outside. This makes China a major uncertainty factor for the future of the region.

The other project carried out by the United States in constructing a new regional order in Asia involved what I call hegemony. I think of hegemony as a kind of structural power rather than as total dominance. Imagine a field, where a number of actors A, B, C, D, and so on are present. Now suppose I organize the field in such a way that I can benefit from everything that each of these actors does in pursuit of their own interests. In this situation, I would hold hegemony over this field. There is nothing particularly mysterious about what I am saying here. Think of the computer software business, for example, and the kind of "built-in" structural power Microsoft enjoys. This is what I mean by "hegemony." The question then becomes: how did the United States organize the Asian regional order to ensure that it enjoyed this hegemony? In simple terms, the key lay with the dream of a life of plenty the United States represented and with faith in the idea that economic growth was the means to achieve this dream. But to explain why this was the case, we will have to look at things in greater depth.

Japan as Number Two

Let us begin by considering Japan, first. What are the general ideas that have informed Japan's Asia policy over the last 50 years?

The first is economic cooperation. In line with U.S. policy to make Japan the workshop of Asia, the politics of productivity informed the overall strategic vision of the Liberal Democratic Party-dominated conservative coalition. As Charles Maier put it, the politics of productivity was a politics aimed at transforming political issues into problems of output and to adjourn class conflicts in favor of a national consensus on economic growth. This politics, which started in earnest in the mid-1950s, was predicated on the conservative pro-business conception of the national interest. Central to this conception were the twin goals of economic growth and industrial transformation. Foreign economic policies were integral to this overall growth. Its commercial policy rested on an export strategy demanding reasonably free access to world markets. Economic cooperation was the name of the game to achieve Japan's policy objectives in the region and beyond. The precise nature of this cooperation has changed over time. Between the 1950s and the 1970s, the two main aims of economic cooperation were to boost exports and procure raw materials. In 1958, for example, a white paper on trade described the objectives of economic cooperation as being to establish a stable market for Japanese goods and to procure a stable source of raw materials. By the end of the 1980s, however, economic development in Southeast Asia was itself the chief objective.

The second is the idea of being "the leader of Asia," to use Prime Minister Kishi Nobusuke's phrase. This needs some explanation. Within the postwar regional order, Japan has played the role of junior partner, as "number two," to the United States. In this sense, Japan has occupied a position in Asia decisively different from the position it had occupied before the war. In its plans for a Greater East Asia Co-Prosperity Sphere, the Japanese empire attempted to construct a new order in Asia with itself as the hegemon or number one. Japan promoted Asianism and called for Asians to "reject the Anglo-American-centered peace." But in the postwar years, a new regional order emerged with the United States as leader. If Japan accepted this order (in other words, unless it was prepared to try to shake off the American hand placed upon its jugular), there could be no question of Japan's rejecting any Anglo-American peace or challenging American hegemony in Asia.

Nevertheless, Japan still occupied a central position of importance as a strategic base for the United States in the regional order. If one chose to regard the United States as existing outside this system, it was therefore possible to speak of Japan as the "leader" of Asia. According to Suehiro Akira, Kishi recalled his purpose in visiting several Southeast Asian countries as prime minister in 1957 in the following terms: "I was planning to visit the United States as prime minister. I did a tour of Southeast Asia first, because I thought that when I was negotiating with the United States I needed to negotiate not on behalf of Japan as an isolated power, but as a representative of Asia." For postwar Japan, this was perhaps the most pragmatic approach to "Asianism" possible. It matched Japan's position as junior partner, without challenging U.S. hegemony in the region, but was enough to satisfy Japanese nationalism.

After becoming prime minister, Kishi Nobusuke meets U.S. Secretary of State Dulles on a visit to the United States (June 21, 1957) (Photo: AP/Aflo)

We can probably understand the diplomatic efforts of Prime Minister Fukuda Takeo with regard to ASEAN in the latter half of the 1970s in these terms. In the 1970s, important shifts took place in the geopolitical and geo-economic tectonic plates in Asia. These are remembered as the two "Nixon shocks" of 1971 (i.e., the announcement that the president would visit China and the decision to cancel the convertibility of the U.S. dollar to gold), the 1973 oil crisis, the anti-Japanese boycotts and riots that took place in Southeast Asia, and the Communist victory in Indochina. Prime Minister Fukuda's ASEAN diplomacy was an attempt to respond to these changes, as well as to the signing of the Treaty of Peace and Friendship with China and the beginning of economic cooperation. There were two main objectives. One was to support ASEAN as a mechanism of regional cooperation and to develop closer relations between Japan and ASEAN. It was from this period that ASEAN replaced "Southeast Asia" as a new regional concept, and that the relationship with ASEAN became a major pillar of Japan's foreign policy. The other objective was to achieve peaceful coexistence between ASEAN and Communist-ruled Indochina and ensure that Southeast Asia did not become a locus for superpower confrontation. This idea failed with Vietnam's invasion of Cambodia, but we would probably not be wrong to see this policy as an attempt to establish Japan as a representative or leader of Asia in Kishi's sense.

The third principle governing Japan's conduct in Asia was the need to coordinate and cooperate with the United States. Given Japan's position as junior partner, this was only natural. For example, in the second half of the 1960s, during the Vietnam War, Japan's assistance to Thailand, Cambodia, Laos, and South Vietnam, as well as its establishment of the Asian Development Bank, were all policies carried out in the interests of bearing a "fair share of the burden" in supporting U.S.-led "free Asia." After Suharto's New Order was established in 1966, Japan provided one-quarter of all aid to Indonesia between 1967 and 1970 and as much as one-third in the first half of the 1970s. This coordination with the United States continued unchanged after the Vietnam War. After Thailand became a "frontline" state following the Vietnamese invasion of Cambodia in 1978, Japan increased its assistance to Thailand substantially, and by the 1980s Thailand was the third-largest recipient of Japanese aid. Japan's assistance to the Philippines also increased following the 1986 People Power Revolution that brought Corazon Aquino to power—this aid was not only used to support the Aquino government but also was used as a political lever to help maintain the presence of U.S. bases in the Philippines.

Needless to say, there were tensions between the three ideas of economic cooperation, Asianism in Kishi's sense, and Japan-U.S. coordination and "burden-sharing." These were inevitable, given Japan's postwar politics of productivity, Japan's fictive centrality to the Asian regional order, and Japan's semi-sovereign status within the Japan-U.S. Alliance. More important, however, is the fact that these ideas have helped Japan pursue its own interests while at the same time fulfilling the need to maintain the U.S.-led order. This circumstance has remained unchanged up to the present, when the domestic political and economic systems in many countries in East and Southeast Asia are undergoing major changes in the aftermath of the 1997 Asian financial crisis. This can be seen in Japan's comprehensive economic cooperation policies since the late 1980s and in Japan's response to the Asian financial crisis.

As is well known, regional economic development in East Asia began in the mid-1980s. Major factors included Japanese direct investment following the Plaza Accord and an expansion of direct investment in newly industrializing economies. The idea of a "flying geese" pattern of economic development became popular, in which Japan took the lead as the first country in Asia to achieve modernization and economic growth, followed by the newly industrializing economies of South Korea, Taiwan, Hong Kong, and Singapore. These would be followed in turn by ASEAN countries such as Thailand, Malaysia, and Indonesia, with China, the Philippines, and Vietnam to join them soon. This pattern of regional economic development led to the idea of an expanded notion of "East Asia," the region encompassing both East Asia (Japan, South Korea, Taiwan, Hong Kong, and China) and Southeast Asia. This idea became meaningful for the first time in Japan in the late 1980s and the early 1990s as this region came to be perceived as the emerging center of the global economy for the twenty-first century. Japan's comprehensive economic cooperation policy took all these expectations into consideration. For Japan, economic cooperation no longer meant merely boosting exports and procuring raw materials. The most important objective of economic cooperation was now defined as promoting regional economic development with Japanese direct investment, Japanese assistance for structural adjustments, infrastructure building, and development of human resources, as well as increased imports from newly industrializing economies and ASEAN countries.

It should be clear by now that the ideas I have mentioned above are all woven into this comprehensive economic cooperation. As Japanese companies have shifted their production bases to other countries in Asia, it is no longer possible to think of the future of Japanese industry within the framework of Japan alone. The idea that Japanese aid should contribute to the business activities of Japanese companies outside Japan's national borders has come to be broadly accepted. It was also understood that making East Asia a venue for U.S.-Japanese cooperation and coordination would contribute to open regionalism. In addition, political stability and economic development in Asia are Japanese interests in themselves. Strategic thinking of this kind therefore led to the idea that Japanese aid should be used to promote economic development by helping to build infrastructure, provide for development of human resources, and nurture financial markets. Underlying all of this is the fundamental belief that economic growth holds the key to solving many problems. This was the basic premise on which postwar Japan's politics of productivity and economic growth was built. The policy of comprehensive economic cooperation was, in that sense, an attempt to extend the politics of productivity and economic growth beyond Japan's national borders and into Asia. If American hegemony is ultimately founded on the dream of a life of plenty and a belief in economic growth as the means to achieve it, then Japan's comprehensive economic cooperation is meant to bring greater stability to the U.S.-built regional order in Asia and not represent a challenge to this order in any sense, however much it might have been criticized by American "Japan experts" like Chalmers Johnson and James Fallows as a second attempt to construct a Greater East Asia Co-Prosperity Sphere.

Has the Asian financial crisis brought any major changes to these circumstances? No doubt the vision that informed Japan's comprehensive economic cooperation policy may no longer appear as convincing as it used to be within the context of a major financial crisis. And there were quite serious disagreements between Japan and the United States regarding the best ways to deal with the crisis. Nevertheless, there was total agreement about the need to return Asia to the path of growth, and it is this that is of primary importance from the perspective of stabilizing the regional system. One wonders whether any major change might have taken place if an Asian Monetary Fund were established in 1997 as Japan had proposed. American officials did not like the idea and worried whether Japan was going hegemonic. But my sense is that it would not have made much difference either way. In those days (as it is now), the United States holds a veto in the World Bank, as Japan holds one in the Asian Development Bank. If the plan had gone ahead, Japan would have acquired a veto in a newly established fund that would have stood alongside the U.S. veto in the International Monetary Fund. The Asian financial crisis did not threaten to change the face of the regional systems, even as it would have provided much needed liquidity to those hit hard by the crisis. Even if the crisis could be said to be comparable in magnitude to the crises of the 1970s, it did not represent a shifting of the tectonic plates along the lines of those that took place in the 1940s.

Nation-State Building from Above

How were the countries of Asia incorporated into the postwar Asian regional order centered on the United States? What problems has the Asian financial crisis revealed in the system? Let's look at the case of Southeast Asia.

After World War II, most of the countries of Southeast Asia achieved independence between the latter half of the 1940s and the 1950s. Some countries, like Indonesia and North Vietnam, achieved independence through revolution, while others like Malaya (Malaysia) and the Philippines were granted independence by the colonial power after a "counterrevolutionary" period. But in all these countries, nationalism was the driving force of the time. Although the United States came up with a triangular trade system involving itself, Japan, and Southeast Asia, and Japan tried to use economic cooperation to promote exports and procure raw materials, Southeast Asian governments did not accept these ideas immediately. Once a state becomes a nation-state, it needs to demonstrate that it belongs to the people. Socialism offered one model for building a national state and economy along these lines. Vietnam and Burma were among the countries that chose this model. Other countries, including Thailand, Malaysia, Indonesia, the Philippines, and Singapore, which had already been integrated into the U.S.-led regional system, generally ended up trying an authoritarian approach to building the nation-state and economy from above. This brought further changes to the modern leviathan states in Southeast Asia, which I will talk about more in the next chapter. What I want to make clear here is that this type of nation-state building from above was closely linked with the integration of these countries into the regional system, and that the two were embedded in an ideological belief in "development."

A good way to understand what this means is to look at the historical origins of developmentalism. Its basic characteristic lies in a combination of nation-state building from above and a belief in economic growth. Suehiro Akira has provided a good explanation of how developmentalism arose as a model in his essay on developmentalism.

In the early 1950s, M.F. Millikan, an economist specializing in the Soviet Union who had served as assistant director of the CIA, and W.W. Rostow, later famous for his "take-off" model of economic growth, were the leading members of a research team at the MIT Center for International Studies working on underdeveloped regions and U.S. economic aid policies. In the 1960s, Millikan and Rostow were appointed presidential advisors on foreign economic policy and national security policy in the Kennedy administration. The findings of their research team were published in 1957 as *A Proposal: Key to an Effective Foreign Policy*.

The proposal argued that for underdeveloped countries to resist international communism and avoid violent revolution within their borders, social reforms driven by economic development were essential. It prioritized the idea that the leaders of underdeveloped countries should take the initiative in carrying forward development programs themselves. The proposal therefore advocated not Western-style individual liberty or economic liberalism but rather a national effort that would unite people of all classes behind the idea of development and a strong leadership role for government in economic policy. In other words, it emphasized a top-down approach to development. Most of the basic conditions of what would later be termed "developmentalism" were already present in this proposal.

Why did things happen this way? Probably for quite simple reasons. At the beginning of the twentieth century, the Netherlands had no choice but to use the state as an agent in its civilizing project. Industrial capitalism of the kind that made Americanization possible in the twentieth century simply did not exist there yet. The circumstances were similar in Southeast Asia in the 1950s and 1960s. The only way to fight back against domestic revolutionary or communist forces was by means of social reforms within that country. The question was: what would be the agent of these reforms? Industrial capitalism did not exist. This meant that governments had few options but to try to cultivate capitalism through top-down development. Developmentalist projects were designed to support this by channeling funds in the desired direction. Given Japan's history of modernization, from the early Meiji efforts to develop industry to the postwar economic recovery, these were the types of projects that most Japanese found easy to understand and sympathize with.

Another factor in U.S. developmentalism is a frequent overlap with the project of Americanization: a tendency to use education to cultivate people who share the same language and think about things in an "American" way, and to enlist these people into institutions of state. I have already discussed this elsewhere, so I will limit myself to a brief example here.

In Indonesia, for example, training of economists began in the early 1950s, with the setting up of a new economics department in the University of Indonesia with a grant from the Ford Foundation. American economists were dispatched as visiting professors, and the previous system, which used Dutch professors giving lectures in Dutch using Dutch textbooks based on the curriculum used in Dutch universities, was replaced by a new system in which American professors lectured in English using English textbooks based on the curriculum used in American universities. After graduation, students were sent to the United States on fellowships from the Ford Foundation to pursue graduate studies. By the beginning of the 1960s, the economics department at the University of Indonesia had become home to a group of Indonesian economists who spoke the same language as their American counterparts.

Following the establishment of the Suharto regime, these economists entered the government as technocrats. With the establishment of government agencies for state-led economic development like the National Development Planning Agency, government development banks, investment committees, and others, many of these technocrats found positions as high-ranking officials in the government and were responsible for the management of Indonesia's economy, through cooperation with the IMF and the World Bank, the Center for International Development at Harvard and other U.S. academic institutions, and consultancy contracts with Lehmann Brothers and other investment banks. Of course, these economists did not have the power to decide everything about Indonesian economic development policies. Nevertheless, there is no doubt that in Suharto's Indonesia, technocrats who spoke the same language as the Americans were incorporated into the state through the government ministries and offices where they worked, which then became a kind of Trojan horse for Americanism. In the 1970s, the dream of a life of plenty and a corresponding faith in economic growth as the means to achieve it gradually became more widely accepted among the population, thanks to successful development and improvements in people's quality of life.

Seen in this way, the sense in which the Asian regional order stands at a crossroads today should be clear. The regional order has not been brought to a state of systematic crisis by the Asian financial crisis. Certainly, there have been differences and tensions between Japan and the United States regarding ways for dealing with the crisis. These came to the surface in Japan's proposal for an Asian Monetary Fund, and Japan's huge financial support for Malaysia and other Southeast Asian countries through the Miyazawa Initiative. The fundamental reason for these differences, in simple terms, is that while stability and development in Asia are in Japan's interests in themselves (because of their FDIs and region-wide supply chains), the economic interests of the United States in Asia are narrower and lie in finance rather than industry. But these differences can be managed and should not threaten the regional order. At issue now is whether the countries hit hard by the financial crisis can rebuild their political and economic systems, get back on the economic growth path, and meet the hopes and expectations their peoples have about a life of plenty. A developmentalist regime gets in trouble when it fails to deliver economic prosperity. What is now being asked in this post-developmentalist era is whether these countries can achieve political stability, economic prosperity, and social peace again in a new, hopefully more democratic way. On this question depends the long-term stability of the region.

CHAPTER SEVEN

Nation-State Building from Above

The countries of Southeast Asia achieved independence in the years following World War II, from the latter half of the 1940s into the 1950s. Some, including Indonesia and North Vietnam, became independent through war or revolutions. Others, such as Malaya (Malaysia) and the Philippines, were granted independence by the former colonizing power after a counterrevolutionary struggle to restore the former regime. Everywhere, once a state became independent, it had to demonstrate in one way or another that it was truly a nation-state that belonged to the people. Socialism provided one model, chosen by countries like Vietnam and Burma. Others, including Thailand, Malaysia, Indonesia, the Philippines, and Singapore, attempted to build a nation-state from the top down, within a regional order centered on the United States as number one and Japan as number two.

Until quite recently, these attempts seemed to be proceeding quite well in many countries, thanks to rapid economic growth. Between 1985 and 1995, for example, almost all the non-Communist countries of the region enjoyed high average growth rates in per capita income: Thailand, 8.4 percent; Singapore, 6.2 percent; Malaysia, 5.7 percent; Indonesia, 6.0 percent. One of the few exceptions was the Philippines, with an average annual growth rate of just 1.5 percent. It is therefore fair to say that in every country apart from the Philippines, there were real, tangible improvements in people's lives, year after year. As long as times were good, the process of building nation-states seemed to proceed smoothly. It was the financial crisis at the end of the twentieth century that exposed the reality that this was not necessarily the case. In this chapter, I propose to look at how modern nation-states have been built in these countries over the past 50 years, and to examine the changes this process caused in the modern leviathan states that were born in the region at the time of Raffles in the nineteenth century.

I mentioned in Chapter Three the lines written in his memoirs by U Nu, the first prime minister of Burma after its independence in 1948, comparing the state he inherited from the British at independence to a car: U Nu unexpectedly found himself thrust into the driver's seat as prime minister. But he had never driven a car before. This would have been bad enough on its own, but the car he had been given was a derelict, with leaks in its gas tank and radiator, and punctures in both front and rear tires. And the road ahead was in terrible condition.

Such was the situation everywhere in the emerging independent states of Southeast Asia in the years following World War II. There were numerous challenges: how to repair the vehicle, how to upgrade the state apparatus into a machine that would follow the intentions of the driver, and how to build a state and government that the passengers could believe in and trust as their own; that this was *their* car, and that the person at the wheel was *their* driver. Several countries adopted the top-down model of nation-state construction. It was tried in Thailand between 1957 and 1973, under the governments of Sarit Thanarat, Thanom Kittikachorn, and Praphas Charusathien; in Indonesia, under Suharto from 1966 to 1998; and in the Philippines, under Ferdinand Marcos from 1972 to 1986. (It has also been the model in place in Malaysia since 1971, under the government of the Barisan Nasional or National Front. However, it is still too early to give an overall account of the model's success in Malaysia, and I will omit that country from my discussion here.) Despite their similarities, the way in which these regimes began and ended differed substantially, as did their accomplishments. Why?

In what follows, I propose to answer this question by concentrating on two main issues. The first is concentration of power. If a state is hostage to a royal family, aristocracy, and a small clique of elite landowners, it is difficult for that state to establish any sense of a supreme shared national interest above and beyond social groups, each pursuing its own private interests. The necessary first step is therefore to construct a strong and competent state that can produce a shared public interest through concentration of power. The second issue concerns the way in which access to this power is widened. If the government succeeds in its top-down effort to establish a state and the economy develops, living standards rise, and access to education is expanded, then sooner or later the people will begin to demand the right to participate in politics. This generally begins with the rise of an urban middle class. This results in the fragmentation of the developmental dictatorship and a shift from an authoritarian regime to a more democratic system of government. Is it possible for states to become embedded in and incorporated into society in the process of these shifts, so that they establish a robust model of authority and legitimacy as nation-states? In what follows, I propose to focus on these two questions as I trace the process of top-down nation-state construction in Thailand, Indonesia, and the Philippines.

Thailand: From Concentration of Power to Expansion of Power

Let us begin with Thailand.

At the end of the 1940s, Thailand under Plaek Phibunsongkhram signed an economic aid and military cooperation agreement with the United States. Helped by generous U.S. assistance, Thailand set about a program of "modernizing" its military and police. This was followed in the 1950s by work to put in place a developmental regime under the Sarit government, in accordance with the recommendations of the World Bank. The Office of the National Economic Development Board and the Board of Investment were established, and together with a Budget Bureau under the Office of the Prime Minister, the government implemented an economic policy based on conservative fiscal policies and private sector liberalization. Economic development in Thailand started under this developmentalist regime, bringing major changes to the bureaucratic state.

Unlike the other countries in Southeast Asia, Thailand/Siam was never colonized. This meant that the modern machinery of state was not transplanted from outside in the form of a colonial state but came about following reforms of the "mandala" type of proto-state headed by the "great kings" of the Chakri dynasty. This process began in the middle of the nineteenth century. In 1855, Siam was incorporated into the British free trade empire following the signing of the Bowring Treaty with Great

Britain. Large areas of the Chao Phraya River basin were brought under cultivation, and rice became a major export commodity. Growing exports led to an increase in state revenue; during the reign of Chulalongkorn (1868–1910), this surplus revenue was used to fund the Chakri reforms that modernized the Thai economy and society. The reforms were wide-ranging, involving central and regional government, the treasury, military affairs, education, transportation, and systems of land tenure. Siam was reorganized into a modern state. To avoid misunderstanding, I should make clear that this process of modernization differed in important ways from the Meiji reforms taking place in Japan at the same time. In Meiji Japan, the reformers built a nation-state from the top down. In Siam, by contrast, the modern state took the form of an absolute monarchy, based on the principle of "*l'état, c'est moi.*" The distinctions between royalty and commoners were strictly maintained, and results-based pragmatism was only permitted within state machinery insofar as it served to strengthen the authority of the king. Under the king, all subjects were treated as equal, without any distinction among the Thai, Lao, or Malay ethnic groups. Immigration from China was encouraged.

This absolute monarchy was later replaced by a bureaucratic state, run by bureaucrats for bureaucrats. At the end of the 1920s, amid the turmoil of the global depression, the international market price of rice plummeted and Siam's state finances collapsed. The government was forced to impose austerity measures, dismissing many bureaucrats and putting others on reduced pay. This increased discontent among the bureaucrats and officers in the armed forces, many of whom resented the fact that they had to remain subordinate to members of the aristocracy because of their commoner status, despite their greater abilities. In 1932, a group of disgruntled bureaucrats and soldiers calling themselves the Khana Ratsadon or People's Party organized a "revolution" and seized control of the government. They abolished the absolute monarchy and introduced a system of constitutional monarchy in its place. However, the so-called People's Party was a secretive group comprising a small number of bureaucrats and military officers who had come together to seize control of the state. It did not enjoy any popular base of support within society.

The "revolution" was in fact a coup d'état, rather than a nationwide experience that led to the birth of new political traditions. The only major change brought about by the "revolution" was that the military and bureaucrats who had previously been incorporated within the absolute monarchy now hijacked the machinery of state and started a shift to a state in the name of "the people"—a concept that had not previously existed in Siam.

This meant that the new bureaucratic state faced a major problem from the outset: the lack of any "nation" in whose name the new nation-state could be legitimized. The bureaucratic state therefore sought its raison d'être in the nationalist ideology of "king, religion, and the nation." In this way, the king and the monarchy survived as symbols of the legitimacy of the state. But the monarchy is an institution different from all the modern political institutions: the king or queen and the monarchy are fused into one (and each king or queen has to reinvent himself or herself to give new meaning to the "national" monarchy). By simply being there on the throne and seeing all the strongmen come and go over decades (from the late 1940s to the 2010s), politically astute King Bhumibol made himself indispensable to and inseparable from the Thai nation-state as successive constitutions defined the Thai political system as a democracy with the king as head of state. Under this new system, the national government was monopolized between the 1930s and the early 1970s by the military and the bureaucrats. Factional disputes became the norm; there were no serious ideological disagreements or any attempt to mobilize students, workers, farmers, or any other social groups. Governments rose and fell as factions converged and fragmented, and coups d'état became regular occurrences. The defining characteristics of this factional politics were the stability of the system itself and the instability of individual governments within it.

The foundations for the social support of this bureaucratic state eventually collapsed, owing to the economic development that took place under its rule. Economic development expanded private sector business groups and the business elites that controlled them, as well as small- and medium-sized entrepreneurs, white-collar workers, doctors, university lecturers, and other professionals, together with students, who between them formed a new urban middle class. At the same time, greater access to education led to the emergence of growing numbers of people demanding the right to be involved in politics. "We are Thais," they claimed, "and the Thai nation-state belongs to us." The student revolution that took place in 1973 was the political consequence of these social changes.

Following this, the trajectory of Thai politics was roughly as follows. First came a period of power-sharing from 1973 to 1988, marked by coalitions that brought military officers, bureaucrats, and technocrats together with entrepreneurs and conglomerates that had sprung up in Bangkok and other cities during the developmentalist period. This was followed by political party rule beginning in 1988. During the power-sharing period, regional "bosses"—who ran construction companies, hotels, and bus companies—came to prominence in provincial cities, and by the mid-1980s they had begun to take control of the political parties that had previously been under the control of the Bangkok elite. This was a major reason for Thailand's entering a period of politics dominated by political parties and the moneyed elite after 1988.

As a consequence, Thai politics has been characterized by two general trends since the 1970s. The first is "democratization," in the sense of broader participation in the political process. To understand the profound impact of the changes this wrought, it is sufficient to compare the military-dominated politics of the 1960s with the party-dominated politics of the 1990s. Also, as has often been noted, this process of democratization has progressed within the context of a repeated cycle along the following lines: coup d'état, constitutional promulgation, formation of political parties, general election, parliamentary politics, political crisis, coup d'état. And it is important to remember that King Bhumibol made himself even more indispensable to Thai politics as the cycle was repeated.

The other characteristic is that of homogeneity within the domestic political structure. Conflicts of interest occur within any society. In Thailand, these have taken the form of antagonisms between Bangkok and the regions, and conflicts of interest between the military, technocrats, the tycoons and middle classes of the capital, and the regional bosses. But in Thailand these conflicts of interest have never led to serious conflicts based on ideology, ethnicity, or religion. This both guaranteed the homogeneity of the political structure and hindered the formation of an all-embracing political party that could bridge these various conflicting interests. As a result, during the period of rule by political parties, the government was often a coalition made up of numerous parties that would be better termed a conglomeration of factions than political parties. For example, when Chuan Leekpai formed his government in November 1997, it consisted of a coalition comprising 211 members drawn from a wide variety of parties: 123 from the Democrat Party, 39 from the Thai Nation Party, 20 from the Social Action Party, 15 from the Khana Ratsadon, 8 from the Solidarity Party, 4 from the Liberal Democratic Party, and 1 member each from the Palang Dharma Party and Thai Party.

In this way, with numerous twists and turns along the way, the process of nation- and state-building in Thailand has proceeded from concentration of power during the development model period to power-sharing and diffusion of power during the period of political party rule. Of course, not everything has gone smoothly. The structure of the Thai economy changed significantly from the 1980s into the 1990s, for example. Against a backdrop of rapid economic development, the gap between domestic investments and savings grew from two to five percent. This was made up for by direct investment and dollar-denominated funds from outside the country. This increased the money supply, causing an economic bubble that finally burst in 1996. There was a rapid increase in bad debt in real estate and consumer loans, and numerous banks and financial institutions collapsed. The Thai baht was affected by the Mexican currency crisis and struggled with currency speculation, and as early as 1996 the International Monetary Fund was already warning the Thai currency authorities to review their policy of pegging the baht to the U.S. dollar. However, it was only in June 1997 that the Thai government finally decided to close the collapsing banks and only in July that it floated the baht on international currency markets and asked for IMF support. Why was the response so slow?

In the 1990s, the government was propped up by large coalitions, and cabinet positions were allocated in proportion to the number of members each party occupied in the coalition. The Budget Bureau set up by the Sarit government to implement development planning became a center for doling out privileges and emoluments, and the role of technocrats in shaping policy was vastly reduced. Vested interest groups began to take the stability of the government hostage in return for protecting their own interests, opposing any policies that threatened their interests with their veto. These vested interest groups split the government into competing factions, each looking to protect its own interests. This hobbled the government's ability to deal with problems and respond to crises.

Seen in this way, it is easy to appreciate the ongoing attempts at reform of the system of party rule. But the most important thing to note is that even at the height of the crisis, Thailand never experienced the rioting, looting, or ethnic and religious violence that happened in Indonesia. One reason is that Thailand is far more socially and culturally homogenous than Indonesia. It is fair to say that this homogeneity abetted successful nation-state construction, and that the homogeneity itself was not the natural result of Thailand's location or history but something that resulted from Thailand's successful construction of a nation-state.

Indonesia: From Concentration of Power to Dispersal of Power

What was the situation in Indonesia?

Beginning midway through 1966, the bureaucratic state was reconstructed in Indonesia under Suharto's New Order regime. Insofar as this was a state run by bureaucrats for bureaucrats, it resembled the bureaucratic state in Thailand. But there were also important differences. In Thailand, the bureaucratic state was transformed into a nation-state beginning in the 1970s. In Indonesia, on the other hand, the bureaucratic state took on the color of a dictatorship under Suharto, until it finally collapsed amid the economic crisis. Today, this crisis threatens the survival of the state itself.

There are probably several reasons for the differences between Thailand and Indonesia. One is the difference in historical origins. The bureaucratic state in Thailand came about as a result of the "revolution" that unseated the absolute monarchy of the Chakri dynasty. In Indonesia, by contrast, the bureaucratic state was born as a nationalist transformation of the colonial, bureaucratic state of the Dutch East Indies. This led to huge differences in the process of transformation. The "revolution" in Thailand did not produce a sense of nationhood. But in Indonesia, a clear concept of nation was born during the struggle for independence from Dutch rule. It was this "nation" that experienced the nationalist movement from the 1910s to the 1930s and provided a foundation of social support to political parties after the period of war and revolution in the 1940s. By the 1960s, parties like the Indonesian Communist Party (PKI) and the Indonesian National Party (PNI) had tens of millions of members and sympathizers. This meant that these political party forces first had to be demobilized from the top down before it was possible to rebuild a bureaucratic state in Indonesia. Suharto achieved this through shock treatment. Between 1965 and 1966, more than 500,000 Communist Party members and sympathizers were killed, arrested, or sent into exile. The experience taught the Indonesian people to fear the state.

Suharto decreed that the central focus of state policy would be stability and development and then legitimized his rule based on his achieving these goals. A schematic summary of Suharto's politics of stability and development might look something like this: political stability → economic development → improvement in people's livelihoods → further political stability. He aimed to form a strong machinery of state, propped up by the support of the armed forces. People were organized into functional groups based on occupation and into neighborhood units, women's associations, the All-Indonesia Union of Workers, groups for agricultural workers, commercial workers, journalists, and so on. Public servants joined Golkar, the governing "Functional Groups," and were required to aid and assist the regime. The political parties were stripped and defanged; workers, farmers, students, and other groups were effectively "depoliticized" and excluded from the political process. Every five years, following its "success" in the "festival of democracy" (as elections were known), Golkar would win another victory, and Suharto was duly reelected as president. This brought about stability, and under this stability the government pushed forward with its development policies. Technocrats trained in the United States occupied strategic positions including chair of the National Development Planning Agency, minister of finance, and governor of the Bank of Indonesia. They ran the development planning and managed the macro-economy and the international debt. The economy grew, thanks to aid from the World Bank and Japan, domestic and international direct investment from the private sector, and the injection of government funding. Industrialization progressed, Indonesia achieved self-sufficiency in rice, and new employment opportunities were created. People's livelihoods improved. This brought further political stability and encouraged people to believe in the legitimacy of the regime. Under Suharto, these policies of stability and development went reasonably smoothly and brought long-term stability to the regime. Why, then, did the regime finally reach an impasse, and why has the Indonesian state now fallen into a state of crisis such as would have been unthinkable several years before?

The impasse itself was perhaps inevitable; it is not surprising that the regime should have come unstuck. But what was important was the way it happened. In Thailand, the structures of the state were not destroyed during the shift from a bureaucratic state to a nation-state. This brought about a shift from concentrated power to a wider diffusion of power. In Indonesia, however, starting in the late 1980s, Suharto began to destroy the state machinery that had been built in the 1970s and early 1980s. In other words, the regime shifted from constructing institutions to deconstructing them; it was no longer building state institutions but tearing them down. Here are two examples.

First is the endemic malaise of family businesses owned and run by Suharto's children. Many Indonesians think of Indonesia as one big family, in which people should help one another like parents and children, or like brothers and sisters. Based on this family ideology, Suharto established foundations, put his business friends in charge of businesses, created funds, and generally looked after his "children" and cronies like a big father figure. But as a way of allocating government funding and projects, this was inherently unfair. Under such a system, a decisive difference immediately arises between people who can depend on their "fathers (*bapak*)" or bosses in some way or form and those who have no one to depend on, even if they might desire it. Nevertheless, until around the mid-1980s, Suharto managed to look after the interests of his lieutenants reasonably well. But as his children grew up and came to own their own business empires, this family ideology came to justify nepotism and favoritism. And naturally enough, if the president and his own children indulge in this kind of behavior, other "public servants" will start to do the same, from ministers, governors, and *bupatis* (regents), all the way down to village heads and other local officials with their own children—until eventually these "public servants" and their children become parasitic, feeding on the state at every level of the hierarchy.

Another example is the rise within the armed forces of Prabowo Subianto, a son-in-law of Suharto. In the 1970s and 1980s, law and order in Indonesia was well maintained through a system of army territorial management that reached from the supreme commander in Jakarta all the way down to the non-commissioned officers seconded to villages around the country. By the end of the 1980s, however, the government faced numerous problems, including independence movements in East Timor, Irian Jaya (the western half of New Guinea), and Aceh, as well as other anti-government protests. The job of "taking care of" these problems was often given to army special forces units under the command of Prabowo, outside the legitimate chain of command. And this was done on direct orders from Suharto himself. For example, around 1990, Prabowo used irregular troops known as "ninjas" against the independence movement in East Timor. These were special commando troops who pretended to belong to underground organizations attached to the independence movement and carried out acts of terrorism, looting, torture, and rape, in an attempt to alienate people from the independence movement and deprive it of popular support. The massacre at Santa Cruz in Dili in 1991 took place at the provocation of these irregular "special forces." Hundreds of people were killed, and the regional military commander and the commander of the East Timor garrison, who were not implicated in the events, were dismissed and forced to take responsibility. Similar events took place in Aceh and in Irian Jaya. Special commandos under Prabowo were also responsible for the kidnappings of activists in 1998 and most likely the shooting of students at the Trisakti University in Jakarta that triggered the riots that led to the downfall of the regime and Suharto's resignation as president.

This meant that the work of demolition or "deconstruction" of the state machinery that had previously been rebuilt by Suharto was already quite advanced by the time the regime fell. As a result, the Republic of

Indonesia fell into a terrible situation. The state became a monster that fed on its people and was consumed at the same time by Suharto and the small Suhartos who modeled themselves on him. The armed forces no longer protected the people but treated them as an enemy. The army was responsible for the deaths of huge numbers of people in East Timor, Aceh, and Irian Jaya. Could such a state somehow maintain its legitimacy as a state that belonged to the people? It doesn't seem very likely. Imagine that you were an Acehnese whose child had been killed by the army for no reason, or that you were a Javanese whose land was suddenly appropriated without warning by a company belonging to the child of the local district chief.

Would you still regard the Republic of Indonesia as "my state" even so? When the state no longer guarantees even the most elementary and straightforward justice, the people (the nation) naturally lose their trust in the state. This situation progressed quietly in Indonesia during the 1990s and came to the surface in a way that was obvious for all to see with Suharto's resignation as president.

Looked at in this way, it becomes clear what is happening in Indonesia today. The changes that have taken place since Suharto's resignation—his replacement first by the interim government of B.J. Habibie and then by the administration of Abdurrahman Wahid—is not the same kind of shift from concentrated power to a wider diffusion of power such as took place in Thailand between the 1970s and 1990s. Instead, it is a swing from concentration of power to dispersion of power such as happened in the 1940s when the Dutch East Indies state was dismantled through war and revolution. But many Indonesians believe that the reasons for the crisis lay with the long dictatorship under Suharto and with an excessive concentration of power. Consequently, many people believe that the key to overcoming the crisis lies in dispersing this power more widely. The government has thus followed a policy of democratization and decentralization. But so long as the state remains a mass of government machinery devoted to racketeering and corruption, democratization and decentralization are likely to decline into nationwide decentralized politics of competing interests and influence-peddling. And if the state does not guarantee basic justice, people will either secure it by their own hands or demand that responsibility for ensuring justice be "restored" to a new state that they feel truly belongs to them. Indonesia today faces a crisis that threatens the continued existence of the nation-state itself.

The Philippines: Systematic Decentralization of Power

Finally, let us look at the situation in the Philippines.

In the Philippines, top-down state building began in 1972, along with Ferdinand Marcos' "revolution from the center." What this "revolution" actually brought, however, was a corrupt authoritarian system built around the personal court of Marcos and his family, and the "new society" collapsed after the People Power Revolution of February 1986. Since then, under the administrations of Fidel Ramos and Joseph Estrada, decentralization of power has been carried out systematically to an extent that would be unimaginable in the other countries of Southeast Asia, with each member of Congress allocated the equivalent of more than ¥100 million from the public purse. How has this happened?

There are probably several major reasons.

The most important of these is historical. During the colonial period, unlike the Dutch East Indies or British Malaya, the Philippines never became a bureaucratic state. In the nineteenth century, Spain was too weak to establish a state apparatus built on centralized power. And when Spain was replaced by the United States at the end of the nineteenth century, the new colonial power had no tradition of bureaucratic rule of its own. Instead, the Americans introduced their own traditions of regional rule into their new colony through a representative assembly. This matched the character of the local Filipino elite well. In the nineteenth century, the Philippine economy was absorbed into the British free trade empire. As a result, beginning in the middle of the nineteenth century, Chinese businessmen started to expand into regional trade in the Philippines. Local Chinese mestizos responded by transforming themselves from regional merchants into high-interest moneylenders, landowners, and producers of commodity goods for export.

In this way, the Filipino elite was born out of the people. They were people whose extensive land holdings gave them a secure economic basis, and whose education in Europe (and later America) made them culturally assimilated. These regional elites went to Manila and controlled the representative assembly as representatives of their respective regions.

This basic structure continued fundamentally unchanged under the framework of presidential democracy after independence. Everywhere, the engine of democratic systems is elections, and what decides elections are votes. As a natural consequence, regional elites built up extensive networks to maintain and cultivate their voting blocs. The military, police, and administrative organs were infiltrated by these competing networks because of these networks' ability to disburse government funding through the representative assembly budgetary process and the control of job appointments.

A system came into being in which power was dispersed to the regions and assemblymen representing the interests of their regions enriched themselves on central public finances through the representative assembly.

In 1972, Marcos declared martial law and attempted to reform this system through a "revolution from the center." He attempted to do this in the following way. First, he dissolved Congress, arrested politicians belonging to anti-Marcos parties, and placed strict limits on political activities. He disarmed private armies, placed strict controls on the media, bolstered the powers of the central government, and attempted to undermine the basis of the regional elites' political and economic power through land reform and other means. Second, he used the armed forces to impose martial law and placed members of the military in important posts in government and government-owned enterprises. The size of the armed forces increased from 55,000 in 1972 to 164,000 in 1977, and to 250,000 by 1984. The defense budget also increased 280 percent between 1971 and 1980. Third, he appointed technocrats to the economic and financial ministries and bureaus, and under their leadership implemented economic development policies based on foreign direct investment. The fourth and final step was to reopen Congress in the second half of the 1970s as a representative system under "constitutional authoritarianism." As a result of elections that were neither free nor fair, the New Society Movement led by Marcos' political allies and technocrats came to occupy an overwhelming majority of seats in the assembly.

Marcos' "revolution from the center" at first glance seems to have a number of points in common with Suharto's New Order regime. But the differences were more important. Suharto's New Order began as a military regime and only became a dictatorship in the late 1980s. By contrast, the Marcos regime was a dictatorship from the outset. This meant that whereas under the Suharto regime military officers were regularly promoted and the army apparatus supported the regime as a major prop of the framework of the state, in the Philippines such a mechanism was never possible. In the Philippines, personal loyalty to the boss trumped loyalty to the organization (or apparatus of state). Whereas Suharto continued at least on the surface to behave as "public servant number one" until the mid-1980s, Marcos was never anything but a "boss," and throughout his time in office the important posts in the army and in government were monopolized by his close relatives and friends.

Marcos' wife, Imelda, for example, was made governor of metro Manila and Human Settlements minister; his cousins Fabian Ver and Fidel Ramos became chief of staff of the armed forces and chief commissioner of the police, respectively; his close friends Juan Ponce Enrile and Roberto Benedict served as defense minister and chairman of the Philippine Sugar Commission, respectively. There were many other examples. During Ver's time as chief of staff, many of his personal connections became "civilians in uniform" in the armed forces, many of them graduates of the University of the Philippines who received basic training in the Reserve Officer Training Corps before being appointed as full-fledged officers in the armed forces.

And the regional elites survived under Marcos. To see how this happened, it is enough to compare Suharto's Golkar with Marcos' New Society Movement. Golkar was a bureaucratic apparatus for mobilizing votes from the people, with the support of the army hierarchy and the Department of Interior. Most of the Golkar politicians in the regions came up through the military or the bureaucracy; most of them had almost no popular base of their own as bosses in the local community. Marcos' New Society Movement was a conglomeration of regional elites with roots in their provinces. As political supporters of Marcos, they used the funding and projects that rained down on them from the central government to maintain and foster their own networks within the framework of the movement. At the same time, they built up their own private armies, under the guise of "private local defense forces" that would supposedly help in the fight against the guerillas of the New People's Army.

These factors meant that in fact Suharto's New Order and Marcos' "new society" were quite different in character. In Indonesia, the regime did at least succeed temporarily at centralizing power and reconstructing a bureaucratic state. Thanks to this, many Indonesians came to understand what a state could mean as an instrument of rule, and still refer to state offices as an "apparatus" of government. In the Philippines, by contrast, all that happened during the Marcos period was that the numerous competing networks of elites that previously existed in the regions were replaced by a single nationwide network with Marcos at its top. This unified network was formed under the influence of a formal strengthening of the state apparatus and centralization of power. To put it another way, the top-down state-building that took place under the Marcos regime was less about constructing a nation-state than about constructing a personal network around Marcos.

But it is impossible to build a personal network successfully in the age of the nation-state. The network started to disintegrate as soon as Marcos fell seriously ill toward the end of the 1970s. Then, after the assassination of Benigno Aquino, Jr., in 1983, the regime went into crisis. Aquino was elevated to the position of national martyr alongside the national hero José Rizal. The Marcos regime became an enemy of the people to rank alongside the Spanish colonial system that had killed Rizal. With this, the regime at once lost all legitimacy in the eyes of the people. This coincided with high oil prices following the second oil crisis, sluggish prices for agricultural commodities, and U.S. Federal Reserve Board Chairman Paul Volcker's anti-inflationary monetary policy. The Philippines' U.S. dollar-denominated international debt position, which had already been deteriorating, suddenly grew even more serious following capital flight, plunging the Manila middle classes into crisis. The Communists and the New People's Army grew rapidly in strength and support. A smooth transition from the Marcos era to a post-Marcos era was in the common interest not only of anti-Marcos groups and the Manila middle classes but also of the Makati business elite, the Catholic Church, and the regional elites, as well as Marcos-supporting politicians looking ahead to the post-Marcos era, the military, and the United States. The revolution of February 1986 was inspired and brought to life by this establishment made up of politicians, the Church, and the business elite through an act of ritual purification under Corazon Aquino, the symbol of national martyrdom.

This meant that in the Philippines, attempts to centralize power never once succeeded, and in the post-Marcos era decentralization of power was systematized constitutionally to an even greater extent than had been the case in the 1950s and 1960s. In the period from 1985 to 1995, the average annual growth rate in per capita income was just 1.5 percent, and people's daily lives hardly improved. The social crisis continues to this day. But the Philippines remained unaffected by a crisis of state such as the one that happened in Indonesia. One reason was that the 1986 revolution had confirmed that the Republic of the Philippines was indeed a nation-state that belonged to the people; the national experience affirmed it. Another is that since the state has never functioned as machinery in the Philippines, people have no experience of any such state and therefore have had no expectations of it from the outset. Instead, they place their hopes in local politicians and more recently anyone (such as movie stars and NGO leaders) with whom they identify.

Seen in this way, it should be clear that the success or failure of attempts to build a nation-state in Southeast Asia has varied greatly from one country to another. One reason for these differences lies in the long-term history of state formation dating back to the mid-nineteenth century. In the case of Thailand and the Philippines, this factor alone goes some way to providing a good explanation. However, the crisis currently underway in the Republic of Indonesia was not due to any such long-term historical consequences, but was caused by the changes that took place in the Suharto regime starting in the late 1980s. Indonesia does have a tradition of rule by the apparatus of state, under a bureaucratic state system. This means that Indonesians place their hopes not in local elites but in the instruments of state. However, over the preceding ten years, the Suharto regime betrayed these hopes. And not only that—it went so far as to destroy the institutions that had been put in place in the 1970s and 1980s. Will it be possible to rebuild the nation-state in Indonesia? The answer to this question will have profound consequences for the future of Southeast Asia as a whole.

CHAPTER EIGHT

Thinking about Asia

Over the preceding seven chapters, I have attempted to address the question I posed at the beginning of this book: how should we think about Asia? I have looked at how the regional order in Asia has been shaped historically by a succession of liberal projects, from the British free trade empire in the age of Raffles to the civilizing mission in the early twentieth century and the U.S.-led "free Asia" project of the postwar era. I have shown the key role played in these projects by the formation and reformation of modern states (leviathans), and I have argued that the role of capitalism as a primary engine driving the formation of a regional order in Asia and the transformation of "East Asia" into a single region are recent developments that date back no farther than the "flying geese" paradigm of economic development in East Asia, with Japan in the vanguard. In this final chapter, I now propose to look ahead. What does the future hold for the regional order in Asia? And what position should Japan occupy in it?

This question is typically considered within a timespan of around half a century. After World War II, Asia's regional systems were reorganized as a new imperial order under the leadership of the United States. Within this order, Japan occupied the position of number two. The standard way of looking ahead to the future would probably be to ask: how is this order changing today, and how should Japan be involved in these changes in the years to come?

But 50 years is not the only conceivable timeframe to use when considering the Asian regional order. The tectonic plate structure that supports the existing order already has a history dating back 200 years, to the time of Raffles. Over that time, a major change has taken place in the position Asia occupies in the global economy. In 1820, Asia (comprising China, India,

Southeast Asia, Korea, and Japan) accounted for 58 percent of the world's total income. But by 1940, following the Industrial Revolution in the nineteenth century and American industrialization in the early twentieth, Western Europe together with Britain and four of its former colonies (the United States, Canada, Australia, and New Zealand) accounted for 56 percent of global income, and Asia's share had fallen to just 19 percent. This trend began to change in the 1960s, with the beginning of a period of rapid economic growth in Asia. By 1992, the region had recovered to represent 37 percent of global income. If this growth continues, by 2025 Asia will again represent 57 percent of global income, bringing it back to the level it was at 200 years ago.

What happens, then, if we look at the regional order that has been born, developed, and matured over the past 50 years, with the United States as number one and Japan as number two, and return it to this longer-term historical context? In what ways can we think of Asia's future? And what should be Japan's objectives within this broader context?

Japan and Asia vs. Japan in Asia

Let me start with a brief overview of the Asian regional order over the past 50 years.

This order was constructed under American hegemony in the years following World War II. The United States had two major strategic objectives. The chief questions facing American policy makers were these: how to deal with the threat of Communism and contain China (and, of course, the Soviet Union), and how to rebuild Japan economically and make it independent as an American ally—while ensuring that it never again became a threat to the United States. The answer was to build a hub-and-spokes security system with the United States as the hub and the U.S.-Japan Security Treaty (and other bilateral treaties) as the spokes and, economically, to construct a triangular trade system linking Japan, Southeast Asia, and the United States.

Within this order, Japan's position was that of the "workshop of Asia" and military logistics base. For Japan, American hegemony was a given, something built into Japan's national security and economic development strategy. Japanese military power was integrated into U.S. power, and economic cooperation became the foundation of the country's relations with the rest of Asia.

Economic development in Asia took place under this system. Under the "flying geese" pattern of development, increasing regionalization saw "East Asia" gradually develop into a single region. The engine driving this movement toward greater regional integration was not international institutions such as ASEAN and APEC but regional economic development. This is why the Asian financial crisis posed such a threat to further progress toward regionalization in East Asia.

What are the structural characteristics of this Asian regional order and of Japan's position within it? A good way to understand what is distinctive about the Asian order is to compare it with the regional order in (Western) Europe. After World War II, the United States faced two strategic challenges in Western Europe: how to respond to the threat of Communism and contain the Soviet Union and how to reconstruct (West) Germany economically as an American ally, while ensuring that it could never again become a threat to the United States and its allies. The United States answered these two questions as follows: in security, by building up NATO as a system for collective defense and security, and rearming Germany within this framework; and economically, through economic integration built around the Franco-German axis. These would later evolve into the European Economic Community, the European Community, and finally, the European Union.

These strategic decisions on the part of the United States resulted in decisive differences between the regional orders in Asia and Europe and the positions occupied within them by Japan and Germany. In Europe, the regional order was based on regional integration as an ideal, and Germany was integrated into the order as "Germany in Europe." Germans defined themselves as Europeans—which is why they were prepared to entrust Germany's future to the European idea, even at the cost of giving up the deutsche mark. In Asia, regionalism as an ideal did not exist, and the order was built on haphazardly developing regions. Japan's relationship with Asia was different from Germany's relationship with Europe. People in Japan did not think of Asia as an integrated whole. The region was thought of in terms of discrete units: here was Japan, there was Korea, over there was Southeast Asia, and so on. Because of this, we do not think of ourselves as "Asians" in the same way that Germans think of themselves as "Europeans," and not even the most dedicated Japanese "Asianist" would consider entrusting Japan's future to the idea of Asianism if that meant surrendering its power over Japan's military or giving up the yen.

For Japan, the desirable outcome has been regionalization that expands Japan's freedom of action within the existing regional order, rather than an Asian regionalism that might constrain its freedom to act as it wishes.

Maritime Asia vs. Mainland Asia

What aspects of the situation come into view if we put the regional order in a longer historical context? The most important thing, and the reason I chose to call this book "Empire of the Seas," is that this new order was built in "maritime Asia" and came about as the result of the dismantling, reorganization, and unification of the British-dominated colonial world of Southeast Asia and the Japanese empire. What do we mean by "maritime Asia"? With a nod to Fernand Braudel's writing on the Mediterranean world, Hamashita Takeshi defines "maritime Asia" in the following terms.

In thinking about Asia, no perspective that concentrates only on the land is sufficient for a full understanding of the region. Historically, one of the major characteristics of the wider region is the existence of a number of maritime zones, stretching from Northeast Asia, through East Asia, and beyond to Southeast Asia and Oceania. The maritime states, regions, and trading cities that exist along the edges of these zones have had a long history of influence on one another. In terms of scale, these maritime zones should be thought of not as huge expanses like the Indian or Pacific Oceans, but as existing on a smaller scale, like the Yellow Sea or the Sea of Japan. An interconnected succession of these maritime zones can be seen to stretch all the way from Northeast Asia to southeastern Australia: starting in the Sea of Okhotsk, and continuing through the Sea of Japan, the Yellow Sea, and the East China, South China, Sulu, Java, and Banda Seas. Then, closer to Australia, come the Arafura Sea and Coral Sea, before finally we reach the Tasman Sea. These maritime zones are surrounded by continents, peninsulas, and islands, and are cut off and distinguished in this way from other maritime areas. The regions located on the periphery of these maritime areas are sufficiently close to influence one another, but far enough apart that they do not become assimilated into one another; thus, they have each maintained their own distinctive traits. They have formed trading areas, around which grew trading ports and cities. Entrepôt cities arose where these spheres overlapped and developed to supply all the conditions necessary for trade, providing markets and residential areas for merchant groups, and issuing currencies.

As this brief description makes clear, this maritime Asia is an Asia that is open to the outside world, a capitalist world linked by trade networks; the idea forms a contrast with the inward-looking, agrarian, "land-based Asia" of mandarins, local gentries, and peasants. But we should not imagine a simple distinction between "land-based" China on the one hand and the rest of Asia as "maritime" on the other. The Konbaung kingdom that flourished in Upper Burma in the eighteenth century, or the Mataram Sultanate in Java, was every bit as inward-looking and agrarian as Qing-dynasty China in the same period. By the same token, in the late Qing and the years of the Republic, Chinese regions like Zhejiang, Fujian (Fukien), and Guangdong (Canton) were just as outward-looking and trade-oriented as contemporary cities like Bangkok and Cebu. The "weather front" that divides maritime and land-based Asia has therefore moved within a given geographical area over the course of history, like shifting pressure troughs on a weather map. This can be seen in the example of the maritime and land-based mandalas that rose and fell in power according to the rhythm of Asian history, or in the way in which the capitalist forces that entered China in the late nineteenth and early twentieth centuries during the age of British-dominated collective imperialism, and then surged into the Chinese interior along railways and rivers from Zhejiang, Fujian, and Guangdong, were then expelled from the land again after World War II, together with the founding of the People's Republic of China.

Empire of the Seas

It was in maritime Asia that the first modern Asian regional order was created. The seas were the areas that Britain colonized first with its naval power. This happened during Raffles' lifetime, when Britain built an informal empire along the line linking Penang and Singapore to Hong Kong and Shanghai. The "informal" empire is a concept used to distinguish the wider sphere of British influence from the formal empire of its colonies, dominions, concessions, and treaty ports. Britain built this sphere of influence by projecting power from its bases in Singapore, Hong Kong, and Shanghai. In this way, Asia was incorporated into the modern international system for the first time, and it was from this period that the project of a regional order began to take shape in Asia, as we saw in Raffles' proposal for a new empire. This project took quite different paths in Southeast Asia and East Asia, however.

What happened?

I have already explained what happened in Southeast Asia. The British free trade empire developed around its center at Singapore. British power was projected from Singapore into the surrounding area, and a network of Singapore-based overseas Chinese expanded like a coral reef across the surrounding seas and islands. The key to the prosperity of this empire was the inflow of immigrants from China. The British Straits Settlements government tamed the network of overseas Chinese through the "respectable Chinese." British hegemony was guaranteed by the toddling leviathan state of the Straits Settlements; in response to the growing British free trade empire based in the settlements, other states based in Batavia in the Dutch East Indies, in Manila in the Spanish-ruled Philippines, and in Bangkok in Chakri-ruled Siam, all began to transform into leviathan states.

The growth of these leviathans brought colonialization to Southeast Asia by the end of the nineteenth century. The whole of Southeast Asia was divided among British Malaya, the Dutch East Indies, the American Philippines, and Siam (Thailand), as well as French Indochina (even though I do not touch on its history in this book), and within territories clearly demarcated by national borders, the authority of the modern states penetrated from the center into the peripheral provinces. The population was disarmed, a "colonial peace" achieved, and work started on the major state projects of constructing ports, laying telegraph and telephone lines, and building railways and roads. Colonial capitalism developed on the foundations laid down by these leviathan states: tin and rubber plantations in Malaya, tobacco plantations in eastern Sumatra, sugar plantations in eastern Java and in Negros, in the Philippines. Everywhere in Southeast Asia, an economy grew based on the export of primary agricultural commodities and mineral resources, and as this economy expanded further into the region, it provided the financial resources to support the leviathan states.

In this way, a colonial world came into being in Southeast Asia. East Asia was different. China disintegrated into a semi-feudal, semi-colonized state, while Japan embarked on an empire-building project of its own.

Why? No doubt there were various reasons, one such factor being historical. In the early modern period during the seventeenth and eighteenth centuries, East Asia followed a different historical course from Southeast Asia. In Southeast Asia, the Portuguese, the Spanish, and the Dutch destroyed the indigenous order and historical rhythm of the region. In East Asia, by contrast, Japan introduced an "isolation" (*sakoku*) policy in 1635, while in China the Qing court allowed maritime trade toward the end of the seventeenth century, after the destruction of the Zheng Chenggong (Koxinga) forces in Taiwan and when it reached the height of its power under the Qianlong emperor.

East Asia thus engaged European forces on its own terms under the hegemony of early modern states and maintained its own indigenous order and historical rhythm in the seventeenth and eighteenth centuries. This was one reason that the incorporation of East Asia into the modern international state system began with the opening of these countries by force in the nineteenth century. This was the meaning of the Opium Wars and the arrival of Admiral Matthew Perry's "black ships" in Japan. The difference between the two countries lies with what happened next.

In China, signs of the decline of the dynastic state were already evident by this time. The typical pattern at the end of a Chinese dynasty was for major rebellions to take place that brought the court to the point of crisis. The rebellions would be suppressed by generals loyal to the emperor, and the court would recover and survive for a few decades more. But the authority of the emperor would collapse in the aftermath of the rebellions and real power would pass into the hands of the generals who had restored peace. The generals would establish their own areas of control and fight for supremacy. Eventually, one would emerge victorious and form a new dynasty.

The dynastic decline as described above, or (to put it in more general terms) the collapse and dispersal of previously centralized power, was already underway in the mid-nineteenth century. China experienced economic prosperity and enormous population growth in the eighteenth century. But the Qing ruling apparatus remained small and dependent on the local elites for governing the population while its economic prosperity was supported by the influx of silver. And signs of trouble were in evidence by the early nineteenth century. With the introduction of opium as the major import, silver started to flow out of China. Rebellions took place one after another. The government relied on "private" armies raised by mandarins and local gentries to suppress these rebellions. It was at this juncture that China was dragged into the modern international system through its bitter experiences in the First and Second Opium Wars. The institutional mechanisms were provided by the British-led treaty port system, which was built on the Western powers' assertion of rights to consular jurisdiction and territorial concessions, the right to trade along the coasts and for foreign shipping, including warships, to navigate freely on the Yangtze River, and the right to fix tariff rates. The Western powers established military and economic bases at strategic points along China's coast and pushed steadily inland in an attempt to bring the surrounding areas under their spheres of influence. This pushed the social foundations of the imperial state, already heavily weakened and undermined, further toward crisis, and accelerated the decline of the Qing power.

But China was so huge that conquering it outright was unfeasible. The newly born leviathan in Hong Kong therefore did not attempt to bring the surrounding sphere of influence under its direct control as had happened as the Straits Settlements grew and colonized Malaya. The concessions in Shanghai remained underdeveloped even in leviathan terms by comparison, as the name Shanghai International Settlement suggests. China was not carved up among the various imperial powers as had happened in Southeast Asia. Under the British-led Treaty Ports system, coastal areas were incorporated into "maritime Asia" and became semi-colonies of a collective imperialism. Meanwhile, the Qing power continued to decline until it finally collapsed in the 1911 Revolution. The dispersion of power reached its height in the Republican era of the 1910s and 1920s, when regional warlords dominated much of the country.

Japan followed a different historical trajectory. Following the "opening" of the country, Japan was incorporated into the British-led modern international system. Shortly thereafter, the Meiji Restoration brought the rule of the Tokugawa shogunate to an end and a process of modern state building and industrialization from above began. Japan left the Sinocentric tributary trade system and became part of the British-led modern international system. Of course, not everything went smoothly. For Japan, this shift meant a civilizational transformation. This was the import of Fukuzawa Yukichi's famous call for Japan to "leave Asia and enter the West." The upheaval left deep scars on the Japanese collective identity, as can be seen in the calls occasionally heard even today for Japan to "leave the West and return to Asia."

Nevertheless, compared to China, Japan made a much smoother entry into the modern international system. From the end of the nineteenth century to the beginning of the twentieth, Japan began building an empire of its own. All this is well known. Following its victory in the Sino-Japanese War, Japan acquired control over Taiwan and joined the British-led Treaty Ports system as one of the major powers. Next, following its astonishing victory in the Russo-Japanese War in 1905, Japan gained control of Russian interests in Manchuria and colonized Korea in 1910; advances into the continent were the keynote of Japan's early empire-building. Not that Japan had no interest in another direction, in the advance southward into "maritime Asia." But by this time the whole of Southeast Asia had already been colonized, and there was no room left for a latecomer like Japan. Japan accordingly expanded its imperial sphere in areas of least resistance; hence, Japan advanced into the continent, into "land-based Asia."

Japan tried to expand on the interests it had inherited from Russia to create an informal empire in Manchuria. This initiative collided with rising Chinese nationalism. In the 1920s, the first steps to build a party state in China built around the Chinese Nationalist Party and the revolutionary army had begun. In 1928, under the leadership of Chiang Kai-shek, China was again reunified, at least formally. This posed a threat to Japan's empire-building in Manchuria; as a result of the Northern Expedition, Zhang Xueliang swore loyalty to Chiang Kai-shek and placed Manchuria under the control of the Nationalist government.

Confronted by this crisis of empire, Japan attempted to separate Manchuria from the rest of China and incorporate it into the Japanese empire. There was a strategic vision behind this idea. The experience of World War I suggested that the next war, when it came, would be an even more total war than the first, which had involved whole nations in the struggle. The crucial problem for the empire was how to prepare for this coming war. Japan decided that the answer lay in developing and exploiting Manchuria and Inner Mongolia.

This was part of the significance of Manchukuo. Another meaning lay in the idea behind the founding of this new state—the idea of "five races under one union." China was a civilization, not a nation. It was unlikely that the Chinese would ever be able to found a modern state; Japan would create Manchukuo, establish its right to rule over the five races, and found a new (Japan-centric) East Asian order. In this sense, Manchukuo was Japan's response to Chinese nationalism.

But the attempts to establish an empire on the continent did not go as expected. Japan became a target for Chinese nationalism, and from 1935 onward, the actions of Japanese troops stationed in China led to growing tensions, until Japan finally embarked on a war with China following the Marco Polo Bridge incident in 1937. The situation quickly ground to a stalemate. The Japanese army had some 700,000 troops in China, but spread as they were around such a huge country, they were barely enough to maintain control of cities and railways, and they never managed to subdue China militarily. And then came what seemed like a golden opportunity. In 1939, war broke out in Europe, and by 1940, under the furious onslaught of German armies, France had surrendered and the Netherlands were under German occupation. The British forces had withdrawn from the continent and a German victory seemed imminent. Opportunistically, Japan moved to take advantage. The French surrender and the German occupation of the Netherlands meant that Indochina and the East Indies had lost their colonial overlords. Both these regions were rich in rice, oil, rubber, tin, and other strategic materials that Japan needed.

Why not incorporate this region into the new East Asian order? The new order was thus expanded to become a Greater East Asia order, and a southward advance added to the ongoing march into the continent. But to open a second front stretching south into the Pacific at a time when the empire was already bogged down on the continent was nothing short of strategic schizophrenia. The word "Greater" in the Greater East Asia Co-Prosperity Sphere is enough to demonstrate the strategic bankruptcy of the Japanese empire.

In the prewar era, the liberal project thus never worked in East Asia. In the 1940s, the tide of chaos in this region turned and began to flow back into Southeast Asia. Japan destroyed the collective imperialism in China during the Sino-Japanese War and dismantled the colonial order in Southeast Asia in the Greater East Asian War. Japan unleashed a wave of "creative" destruction that brought the colonial world in Southeast Asia to an end. Meanwhile, during the war the Chinese Communist Party expanded its power. Having started the war with 40,000 members and an armed force of 50,000, by 1945 it had swollen to a total membership of 1.21 million, and the Red Army had 910,000 soldiers, as well as 2.2 million militia and 10 million members of the self-defense corps. The civil war ended in victory not for Chiang Kai-shek's nationalists but for the Communist Party. Mao Zedong believed that peasants could build prosperous lives for themselves through their own efforts, and that the strength of the peasants would make China into a rich and prosperous nation that would never again be invaded by foreign powers. With the establishment of the People's Republic of China, China became inward-looking and agrarian again, and an anti-capitalist order was built that was distinct from maritime Asia.

Following these tectonic shifts, from the latter half of the 1940s to the early 1950s, the United States constructed a new hegemonic order in Asia. The basic principle was to contain the peasantist order of land-based Asia in China and to link Japan, Southeast Asia, Korea, and Taiwan to the United States in maritime Asia. Japan became the object of the liberal project for the first time, and the United States set about building a new regional order in Asia with Japan, which supposedly now "shared values" with the West, as a junior partner to the West.

Looking Ahead

Today we live in a regional order with the United States as number one and Japan as number two. Asia is no longer divided into maritime and land-based zones the way it was during the Cold War. Even if China cannot yet be said to have been fully incorporated into the regional order, it is far more open than it used to be. What is likely to happen in Asia in the years to come?

There are probably at least three points we need to consider.

First is the question of American hegemony in East Asia. So long as Asia remains under American hegemony, the regional political and economic system with the United States as number one and Japan as number two is not likely to collapse. The question is whether the United States has the will and ability to maintain its hegemony in Asia in the long term.

The basic principle of American policy in Asia is that no other hegemon be allowed to take the place of the United States. American hegemony is backed by such resources as military might, economic power, intellectual capability, and social systemic vitality. There is probably no need to worry that the United States is going to give up its hegemony in Asia, or lose its ability to maintain it, for the foreseeable future.

But what would happen if a country came to prominence and tried to challenge American hegemony in the region, as Japan did in the 1940s? Just to be clear: Japan does not have the ability to replace the United States. Indeed, it would be foolish even to attempt it. The wild card here is China. Will it really happen that China will take the place of the United States as the hegemon in East Asia one fine day in the twenty-first century, as some people predict? To consider this question properly, we should think about what it would mean in concrete terms for China to be hegemonic in East Asia. This would involve restructuring the East Asian regional order with China at the center. What would this mean? Firstly, in terms of security, it would mean the withdrawal of all American bases from the East Asian region and the replacement of the U.S. Seventh Fleet by Chinese squadrons patrolling a vast maritime region from the Sea of Japan and the South China Sea all the way to the Indian Ocean. Economically, China would become a leader in technological innovation, China would become the world's largest market, and China would take control over East Asia's energy supply. Is it possible for these things to happen? I suppose it is not entirely out of the question. But we probably needn't expect it to happen any time soon or in the foreseeable future.

The second question is the integrative potential of the current regional order, about which I have already written. During the Asian financial crisis of the past two years, a clear historical trend has emerged of suggesting that the age of authoritarian developmentalist regimes is coming to an end, to be replaced by an era of democracy. This does not suggest a systemic crisis in the Asian regional order. The United States and Japan are in agreement about the need to maintain the stable regional order, even if there have been disagreements between them about how to surmount the crisis. The question here is the periphery. The Asian regional order depends on a shared belief that it is possible to bring about a life of plenty by participating in this order, and that doing so further brings political stability and social peace. In this sense, resolving the financial crisis is the key to stabilizing the regional order in Asia. This is already happening in South Korea, Thailand, and other countries. But this is not the only issue, and not even the most important one. For the past 200 years, during the age of British dominance and now during the American era, the basic foundation of the Asian regional order has been the modern state.

But there are substantial differences in character between the modern states in Southeast Asia and those in East Asia. In Japan, the modern state was created from above as a nation-state. In South Korea and Taiwan, too, the construction of nation-states has progressed smoothly over the past 50 years. But the situation in Southeast Asia is different. As we have seen, in this region, the overseas Chinese network acted as the ally of the modern state from the birth of the first leviathans. Together with the growth of the colonial state, what emerged was a plural society in which the various groups that made up a given society did not share any common social purpose. While economic development was going well, it was not clear just how serious a problem this was. The financial crisis has made it evident. What do I mean by this?

Compare the situations in Thailand and Indonesia. Over the past two years, in the midst of the financial crisis, Thailand has not seen any riots or looting. This is because the society was stable to begin with. In Indonesia, on the other hand, fragmentation and diffusion of power started with the collapse of the Suharto regime. Democratization and decentralization, however, brought darker problems to the surface: radical Islamist challenges to the Republic, sectarian conflicts in Ambon, ethnic violence in Kalimantan (Borneo), and independence movements in Aceh and Irian Jaya plunged the country into a crisis that threatens the collapse of social order and the break-up of the Republic. It became clear that in a multi-ethnic, multi-religious plural society like Indonesia with no common shared social purpose, once people lost their faith in the state, there was no social solidarity to support and maintain social order. We do not yet know how this situation will develop in the future. But looking at how precarious the nation-state building project in Indonesia is, it will not do to pretend that the dispersion of power simply means democratization and decentral-ization. It would be complacent to assume that a state in Southeast Asia cannot break apart or that social order cannot collapse.

I do not believe that the region will see the return of mandala states ruled by Malay kings like the ones Raffles knew. But it is quite possible that within the network of the formal states, areas which are quite autonomous from such metropolitan centers as Jakarta and Manila will come into being, and that these will be linked by various networks across national borders. Here and there within these regions there may well be a collapse of order.

The third and final question concerns China: not whether China has the potential to rise as a superpower. As I have already said, there is no need to consider this possibility, at least for the time being. Rather, we should think about the potential of what we might call the Greater China sphere of influence. Over the past 200 years, with numerous ups and downs and twists and turns, the network of overseas and ethnic Chinese from Fujian and Guangdong has put down deep roots throughout Southeast Asia, and an alliance with the overseas Chinese has been of decisive importance in the running of a country's economy, as seen in the case of the British free trade empire in the days of Raffles (a success) and today's Indonesia (a failure). If the Asian economy continues to develop, there will probably be no major change in these circumstances for the time being. The real question here is what significance this overseas Chinese network will have for the future of China.

In China, empires have always been built on the control of the land-based society. The same is true of the People's Republic of China today. In the historical dynasties, imperial power was built on mandarin and local elite control of the peasant society; and in the People's Republic, it is control of the vast rural society by the Communist Party that provides the foundation of state power. Not once has China known a capitalist state; prosperous business and the development of a market economy have always threatened and undermined the very foundations of a Chinese state, whether dynastic or republican. Chinese history demonstrates the truth of this. Several times over the past five or six hundred years, the maritime region that stretches from the Japanese archipelago and the Korean Peninsula through Zhejiang, Fujian, and Guangdong to Southeast Asia has produced an age of commerce. And each time, China has eventually been destabilized. From the fifteenth to the seventeenth centuries, *wakō* pirates wrought havoc and the Ming declined; during the imperialist age of the nineteenth and twentieth centuries, the Qing became semi-feudal and semi-colonized. This is no coincidence. In an age of commerce, power derives from material wealth. This power differs from land-based power. This is why merchants and pirates threatened the control of the Ming, and why overseas Chinese in Southeast Asia at the end of the Qing dynasty supported Sun Yat-sen's revolutionary movement. Today, we are living in a new age of commerce, one that began at the end of the twentieth century.

In this age of commerce, will China be able to create a capitalist state and a market economy, that is, an open political and economic system capable of converting market economy dynamism into national power and providing a life of safety, plenty, and freedom? The prospects do not seem very bright.

What should Japan aim to achieve in the years to come?

For the past 50 years, the Asian regional order with the United States as number one and Japan as number two has been quite a comfortable one for Japan. Under this system, Japan's safety and prosperity have been guaranteed by the U.S.-led security system and by the triangular trade linking Japan with Southeast Asia and the United States (and Western Europe). And for the past 50 years there has been no need for Japan to worry about whether it should advance into the continent or go south (the choice between land-based and maritime Asia).

And over the past 50 years, as we can see from Kishi's espousal of a new kind of Asianism within the U.S.-led regional order, Japan has found a way to effectively harmonize internationalism and Asianism. Japan has no wish to change such a comfortable system; building a new order in Asia with Japan at its head is neither desirable nor feasible. What is important for Japan is to ensure the systemic stability of the Asian regional order that exists here and now, strive to achieve regional prosperity, and look to expand Japan's freedom of action within this system.

What should Japan's policy be? Japan's position in Asia is different from Germany's position in Europe. For now, Japan's relationship with the rest of Asia is one that can be characterized as "Japan and Asia," even though it is fast changing into "Japan in Asia." Since the mid-1980s, Japan has promoted regionalization by taking the lead in the flying geese paradigm of economic development and investing heavily in building supply chains. But we will not entrust our future to the idea of regional identity in the way that Germans entrusted their future to the European idea. And any idea of expelling Anglophone influence from Asia and gambling everything on Asianism would be the wild ravings of a lunatic. Japan should aim for harmony between internationalism and Asianism and for the stability of the Asian regional order. We should do our best to gradually change the economic, social, and cultural parameters of the relationship between

Japan and East Asia through the expansion and deepening of exchanges and economic, cultural, intellectual, and technical cooperation, and to build a framework within the regional order that will be in the interests not only of Japan but also of South Korea, Taiwan, and the countries of Southeast Asia. Japan should continue to promote regionalization which would further embed Japan in Asia in a way that is different from Germany in Europe.

AFTERWORD

Almost exactly ten years have passed since I first started to think of Asia as a regional system, and embarked on this attempt to understand Asia by thinking about how that system came into being, and the changes it has undergone over the centuries since.

I spent almost a decade teaching at Cornell University in Ithaca, New York, from 1987 to 1996. Between 1990 and 1991 I spent a year in Jakarta, and when I returned to Ithaca in the fall of 1991, I noticed that something had changed. Various regional studies programs were offered at Cornell at the time: Southeast Asian studies, East Asian studies, and so on. And one day I noticed that one of these, the Soviet Union and Eastern European studies program, had disappeared. With the fall of the Berlin Wall in 1989 and the collapse of the Soviet Union in the revolutions that swept across Eastern Europe, the concept of the Soviet Union and Eastern Europe as a region had lost its meaning.

This came as a shock. Not that I was worried that one day Southeast Asia too might suddenly vanish, or that the Southeast Asian studies program might disappear in the same way. But it was clear that Southeast Asian studies could not exist without the concept of "Southeast Asia." I had been aware of the truth of this obvious statement before, but it was brought home to me vividly now as I watched researchers who until recently had been specialists in "the Soviet Union and Eastern Europe" frantically trying to reinvent themselves and relaunch themselves as specialists in ethnicity, democratization, and/or transitioning to market economies.

It was this experience that spurred me to consider anew how we should think about regions.

In the case of Southeast Asian studies, the question had always been an important one. The reason was simple: "Southeast Asia" itself was an empty term with no fixed meaning. It was first used in the years after World War II. The consensus among Southeast Asian historians is that the term was first applied in an official context to the "South East Asia Command" under Louis Mountbatten during the war. But this was a British usage. In the United States, the term "China and its vicinities" referred to the area encompassing China and what we think of as Southeast Asia today, and it was not until 1949 or 1950 that the term "Southeast Asia" was first used in Washington. Why was this?

It was probably because of the establishment of the People's Republic of China in 1949 and the outbreak of the Korean War the following year. "China and its vicinities" presumably no longer felt like an appropriate way in which to refer to the region, and "Southeast Asia" was used as a way of separating the "vicinities" from China. In other words, the term was born at the beginning of the Cold War and became part of the conceptual apparatus that underpinned U.S. strategy in Asia during the Cold War era.

All of this is well known. But what was more important was what happened next. Once the term was in use as part of the conceptual apparatus in the U.S. Asia strategy, it became clear that there were no specialists in this field. The reason was obvious: there could be no experts on a collection of countries that had never been regarded as a single region before. A need was felt for more research on Southeast Asia, and Southeast Asia studies programs were established at Cornell, Yale, and other universities, funded by research and education grants from the government and private foundations. "Specialists" in Southeast Asia were hired as teachers, and courses were set up to teach Indonesian, Thai, and the other languages of the region. Supported by generous funding and scholarships, the work of training Southeast Asian specialists began. Before long, these programs started to produce Southeast Asia specialists who were comfortable with the languages of Southeast Asia. These specialists carried out fieldwork in Southeast Asia and obtained their doctorates in various disciplines. These developments took place in the 1950s and 1960s.

In this way, the new field of Southeast Asian studies was established. But in fact, the labeling was misleading. Southeast Asia is home to numerous languages: Thai, Vietnamese, Tagalog, and Indonesian, to mention only a few. It was impossible for any single scholar to acquire all these languages and become a specialist in Southeast Asia in the true sense of the word. The reality was that most scholars were interested in a narrower area—Thai history or Indonesian politics, for example—but since there were no jobs for specialists in these fields, they labeled themselves as Southeast Asia specialists instead. Naturally, this caused a degree of discomfort and led to something of an identity crisis among Southeast Asian scholars. For these reasons, the questions "What is Southeast Asia?" and "How should we think about regions?" became important issues in the field.

What could be done? One attempt to resolve the question was the textbook, *In Search of Southeast Asia*. Of course, a book like this could not have been written by one person alone. A number of experts on the history of Thailand, Indonesia, the Philippines, Burma, Malaysia, and Vietnam came together as a group to produce this book. But reading it through to the end was not enough to enable a reader to "find" Southeast Asia. Simply cobbling together the histories of single countries was not enough to produce a unified history of Southeast Asia as a whole.

This much was clear. Some people who could see more clearly, such as Benedict Anderson, who became an international academic star after the publication of his book *Imagined Communities*, to which this book owes a lot, did not pose the question: "What is Southeast Asia?" He knew quite well that Southeast Asia was a term without any fixed content. Anderson accepted this and decided to ask questions about world history from a Southeast Asian perspective. This led to his books *Language and Power* and *The Spectre of Comparisons*.

Personally, I was not satisfied with either of these positions. It was certainly true that Southeast Asia had been created as an empty term. But it was also true that over time the term had come to take on a meaning of its own. It was because people tried to treat the region as a single stable structure that they either ended up searching for something that could not be found, or else dismissed the concept out of hand.

What to do? Even if it was not possible to treat the region as a structure, given unity by certain stable commonalities (civilization and culture, for example), why not try to look at it in terms of regionalization—in other words, why not look at the historical processes by which the region had come into being, developed, and matured? In this way, even if the concept of "Southeast Asia" disappeared one day, the field would be able to study that process objectively. This line of thought led to the basic idea for this book: to examine the birth of regional systems within maritime Asia and the changes they had undergone, centered on the formation of two informal empires, and to look at the macro-comparative history of modern states in Southeast Asia and their relations with Japan in this context.

The essays that make up this book were originally serialized in *Chūō Kōron*. They were prompted by the receipt in 1998 of a grant-in-aid for a Centers of Excellence research project led by me, entitled "The Making of Regions: Proto-Areas, Transformation, and New Formation in Asia and Africa" at the Center for Southeast Asian Studies (CSEAS) and the Graduate School of Asian and African Area Studies (ASAFAS), Kyoto University.

In the pieces I published in *Chūō Kōron*, I tried to write about the foundations of this project and my ideas about the region in accessible terms for a general audience. I am grateful to *Chūō Kōron* for the opportunity to present my ideas to a wider readership and am delighted to see them appear in book form now. It will be clear to anyone who reads the book that I incurred a debt of gratitude to many people in the course of writing it. Miya Kazuho and Hayama Ryuhō were ideal sounding boards and conversation partners in thinking through the ideas behind the original essays. For the concepts of maritime Asia, regional systems, and the overseas Chinese network, I drew on the work of Hamashita Takeshi. Much of what I say on states, societies, and economies in Southeast Asia I owe to Benedict Anderson and Hara Yōnosuke; likewise, on the comparison between Japan and Germany, Peter Katzenstein; on developmentalist regimes, Suehiro Akira; on population gazettes in Southeast Asia, Tsubouchi Yoshihiro. During the editing process, I was fortunate to be helped by Kuroda Takeshi, my editor at *Chūō Kōron* magazine, and Ishikawa Kō of the *Chūō Kōron Shinsho* editorial department. This book is respectfully dedicated to the memory of two departed friends: Professor George Kahin and Uehara Takashi.

Shiraishi Takashi
August 2000

ADDENDUM: 2020

The regional order in Asia has undergone significant developments since this book was first published in 2000. Instead of writing another chapter or two to update the book, here I will touch on some of these developments, which are particularly important in understanding how the regional order is being transformed.

The most notable development, both globally and regionally, is the rise of emerging states and economies. The share of the global economy accounted for by such countries has more than doubled between 2000 and 2018. The standard of living in these countries has also improved significantly. And Asia, a region of emerging countries, has become the center of global economic growth. The ascent of China is especially remarkable as its GDP, whose share of the global economy was less than 4 percent in 2000 (in U.S. dollars), rose to 16 percent in 2018. The global economic shares of the ASEAN-5 (Indonesia, Malaysia, the Philippines, Singapore, and Thailand) and India, which stood at 1 percent and 1.4 percent, respectively, in 2000, rose to 2 percent and 2.6 percent in 2018. Japan's share, which stood at some 15 percent in 2000, fell to 6 percent in 2018. As economies expand, government revenues increase and military spending grows. If U.S. military spending were to be set at 100, then Chinese military spending increased from 4 to 39 from 1988 through 2018. India's military spending exceeded Japan's military spending for the first time in 2015. As emerging countries rise, the balance of power shifts fast, especially in Asia.

As discussed in previous chapters, the Cold War provided a comfortable international environment for Japan. While Japan lost a disastrous war as Germany had, Japan was not divided as Germany was, nor did it find itself at the forefront of the Cold War, as did Germany. Under these circumstances, the tacit social contract between the state and the people in Japan (and in Germany) was revised. In the United States, the state promises the people "a life of plenty and freedom." China promises "a life of plenty and security." Yet neither state hesitates to use their might as a great power. In contrast, Japan has discarded its great-power ambitions. Instead, the Japanese state promises its people "a life of plenty, freedom, and security." During the Cold War, Japan relied on the Japan-U.S. alliance and pursued high economic growth to ensure the prosperity, freedom, and security of the Japanese.

By the 1990s, region-wide economic development was a fact of life in the area from Japan and South Korea, via the Chinese coastal regions, Taiwan, and Hong Kong, to Southeast Asia. Expanding transnational production networks, with Japanese and multinational companies as drivers, had led to de facto regional economic integration. Following the East Asian economic crisis in 1997–1998, China emerged as "the workshop of the world." The triangular trade system that had hitherto been made up of Japan, the rest of Asia (including China), and the United States (plus Europe) was transformed into a new triangular trade system made up of China, the rest of Asia (including Japan), and the United States (plus Europe). The regional production networks expanded farther, free trade agreements (FTAs) were concluded, and there was de facto and institutional economic integration. Japan's relationship with Asia was no longer "Japan and Asia" but "Japan in Asia."

As a result, a structural tension between the East Asian security system and the regional trade system has come to the fore in the twenty-first century. While China is economically integrated into the East Asian and global economies, it exists outside the U.S.-led regional security system. This is the source of the tension, a tension which will only increase as China rises and asserts itself. The U.S.-led hub-and-spokes system remains a foundation for regional security. Yet this is no longer acceptable to China. The intensifying U.S.-China rivalry will increase pressure to revise regional production networks and transform the trade system.

Unlike the Cold War era, Japan now stands at the forefront of the U.S.-China arena. Yet compared to the Cold War era, Japan is no longer an economic superpower. It is now a mid-rank power with fewer resources than it used to have. This explains why the Japanese government, both under the Democratic Party of Japan and the Liberal Democratic Party, has undertaken policy initiatives to strengthen Japan's alliance with the United States, aligns itself more closely with its partners to build a network for security cooperation, expands the country's regional framework from the Asia Pacific to the Indo-Pacific, and concludes the Comprehensive and Progressive Agreement for Trans-Pacific Partnership (CPTPP, also known as TPP-11). Aware that China cannot be contained, Japan, with the United States and its allies and strategic partners, continues to hedge the risk of China's unilateral attempt to change the regional order by force while engaging China in the fields of multilateral norm- and rule-building as well as cooperation in areas of mutual and regional benefit, including infrastructure development.

In the immediate post-Asian financial crisis days of 1999–2000, when this book was being written, many people, myself included, wondered and worried whether Indonesia would turn into a Yugoslavia, in danger of breaking up owing to ethnic and religious tensions; or a Pakistan, subject to periodic military intervention and the rising jihadist threat; or a Philippines, democratic but with insurgencies simmering in the provinces and a weak and stagnant economy. None of these scenarios have come to pass.

Indonesia remains united. Though rising Islamism is a political threat, the country is at peace with itself except for small-scale insurgencies in Papua. It has seen five free, fair, and peaceful parliamentary elections and four direct presidential elections over the last twenty years. Indonesia's GDP per capita (in national currency at constant prices) increased by 46 percent in the 2010s.

Nor is it fair to refer to the Philippines as a basket case of flawed democracy and economic stagnation. It is true that after the two successful People Power Revolutions and an unsuccessful urban underclass revolt, politics there has sunk into a morass of electoral politicking dominated by professional politicians and sectoral activists. But the Philippine GDP per capita has grown by 42 percent in the 2010s, and its economy—stabilized by the remittances of diasporic Filipinos and powered by domestic consumption and a thriving English-speaking business process outsourcing sector—is the best performing among the ASEAN-5 in recent years.

By contrast, Thailand and Malaysia, the two states often referred to as the best performers in economic development in the 1980s and 1990s, have done less well in the post-Asian financial crisis era. Malaysian politics, especially under Prime Minister Najib Razak, got bogged down in corruption in the post-crisis years and is now adrift. The country saw its GDP per capita increase by 36 percent in the 2010s but is unlikely to achieve its objective of joining the club of advanced economies by 2020. The Thai economy performed even more poorly, posting 23 percent GDP per capita growth in the same period. Its politics is mired in stagnation, with the military elite in power and the monarchy under the new king becoming increasingly absolutist.

China's quest for hegemony and the U.S.-China rivalry have come earlier than I anticipated when I wrote this book. Beginning with its reform and opening in the late 1970s, China had long accepted United States hegemony in the region and had chosen to pursue its economic development within the U.S.-led regional and global order. And China has experienced remarkable economic development. It joined the World Trade Organization in 2001, became the world's largest foreign currency holder in 2008, the world's largest trading nation in 2009, and overtook Japan to become the world's second largest economic power in 2010. With China's rise as an economic superpower and the attendant growth in self-confidence of its people, the great power nationalism of "China is greater than any other country" came to be accepted as a matter of course in China.

This was made clear with the arrival of Xi Jinping as General Secretary of the Chinese Communist Party and Chair of the Party Central Military Commission in 2012, and President in 2013. He has concentrated decision-making power in himself and embarked on challenging the U.S.-led regional system and on establishing a dedicated sphere of influence for China, in the name of achieving the "China Dream."

In response, the United States has shifted its China policy from engagement and hedging to strategic competition. The 2017 U.S. National Security Strategy determined that "China seeks to displace the United

States in the Indo-Pacific region, expand the reaches of its state-driven economic model, and reorder the region in its favor," and that China aims to impose its will on neighboring countries, limit sovereignty, and become the regional leader by investing in infrastructure, expanding trade, amplifying military power, building and militarizing artificial islands in the South China Sea, and issuing military threats.

No doubt China is building its own Sinocentric world in such fields as geopolitics, data circulation and communications systems, advanced and emerging technologies, and trade and investment (including with emerging and developing countries), while spending heavily in military modernization and science and technology development. But this is not a new Cold War. There is practically no risk of thermonuclear war between the United States and China. Given the integration of China into global economics, it is unlikely that the global economy will decouple to the extent that it did during the Cold War era.

It is also a mistake to think that the intensifying U.S.-China rivalry will force other nations to make a choice between Washington or Beijing. All the states in the region—including those identified as U.S. allies and partners—are trying to balance the twin goals of national security and economic prosperity. The U.S.-led security system underpins regional peace and stability. China's growing wealth offers all countries economic prosperity as an expanded market and as an important source of investment funds. Japan and Australia, the region's most prominent U.S. allies (as well as Taiwan), remain closely aligned with Washington when it comes to defense, technology, and telecommunications. South Korea, by contrast, is going its own way, shying away from even talking about a "free and open" Indo-Pacific.

More nuanced are the foreign-policy moves from individual Southeast Asian states as they attempt to maintain as much freedom of action as they can. While seizing the opportunities for economic gain offered by China, many ASEAN states are hedging their political and security risks by aligning themselves with the United States.

Three factors largely inform this balancing strategy. The first is the position individual ASEAN states occupy in the regional security system, which often hinges on whether a member state has a territorial dispute with China over the South China Sea and whether it can take the U.S.-led security system as a given on which to build its own national security policy. The second is the degree to which each country is embedded in the regional and global economy, and how economically dependent it is on China. The third is whether there is dynamic circulation of elites in each country.

Of the five maritime states—Brunei, Malaysia, the Philippines, Indonesia, and Singapore—that rely on the U.S.-led system for their security, four are in conflict with China either over territory or access to their Exclusive Economic Zones. All five states are also well-integrated into the global economy. Four—Indonesia, the Philippines, Singapore, and Malaysia—have significant elite circulation, making it difficult for China to form enduring politico-business alliances that would reshape their political economies.

Vietnam, a one-party state that cannot rely on the United States for security, nevertheless has territorial conflicts with China and worries about becoming too economically dependent on Beijing. This explains Vietnam's cautious engagement with the United States on security issues, as well as its attempts to enhance security cooperation with Russia, India, and Japan, and its participation in the Trans-Pacific Partnership Agreement (TPP-11). Thailand, in contrast, is a U.S. ally without any territorial conflicts with China. Facing a benign international environment with an economy well embedded in global supply chains, Thailand can have its cake and eat it too. The other three mainland ASEAN states—Cambodia, Laos, and Myanmar—have no territorial conflicts with China and are wedded to a system wherein the political and business elites are almost entirely dependent on Beijing. These factors combined explain why ASEAN states have diverging geopolitical and economic interests and why China might be successful in establishing its sphere of influence in parts of mainland Southeast Asia.

In view of all these developments, it is not entirely unreasonable to see the region as bifurcating into mainland Asia and maritime Asia. Regional supply chains, finance, and communications and information technology may be decoupled along similar lines. The question is how extensive such decoupling will be, what its impact on the regional system will be as the rivalry between the United States and China intensifies, and how much political and economic space for maneuver, if not freedom of action, all of these middle and smaller states will have in the coming years.

NOTES AND REFERENCES

CHAPTER ONE: RAFFLES' DREAM

A good biography of Raffles is C. E. Wurtzburg, *Raffles of the Eastern Isles* (Singapore: Oxford University Press, 1984; first published 1954). In Japanese, Shinobu Seizaburō's *Raffuruzu-den, Igirisu kindaiteki shokumin seisaku no keisei to tōyō shakai* [A Biography of Raffles: The Formation of British Modern Colonial Policy and Oriental Society], (Tokyo: Heibonsha Limited, Publishers, 1968, first published 1943), remains worthwhile, despite being written from a perspective that seems outdated today, as its title suggests. Tsurumi Yoshiyuki's *Marakka monogatari* [Tales of Malacca], (Tokyo: Jiji Press Ltd., 1981), also contains a chapter on Raffles. Tsurumi comes down quite hard on Raffles, describing him as "a schemer who used his local knowledge to achieve his own objectives, sometimes openly, sometimes furtively: neither was his knowledge as profound as he allowed himself to believe and trumpeted to other people." It is remarkable how people can read the same sources and evaluate the same person in such markedly different ways. Nigel Barley's *The Duke of Puddle Dock: Travels in the Footsteps of Stamford Raffles* (New York: Henry Holt, 1992) is a travelogue in which the author visits places in Southeast Asia associated with Raffles, but the book is rather glib and hard to recommend. Today, the Hotel Equatorial stands on the site of the government house in Bandar Hilir where Raffles stayed during his time in Malacca. Two centuries of land reclamation and redevelopment mean that the site presents views of the city today that are quite different from what they would have been in Raffles' time.

For Abdullah bin Abdul Kadir's autobiography, in the original Japanese edition of this book I drew on the Japanese translation by Nakahara Michiko, *Abudurrā monogatari, aru Marē-jin no jiden* [The Tale of Abdullah: Autobiography of a Malay], (Tokyo: Heibonsha Limited, Publishers, 1980). Chapter 6 of the book contains Abdullah's descriptions of "Tuan Raffles." Abdullah's book *Hikayat Abdullah* [Life of Abdullah] is an excellent introduction to Malaya and Singapore in the nineteenth century. The citations in this English-language edition are instead taken from "The Hikayat Abdullah," trans. by A.H. Hill, *Journal of the Malayan Branch of the Royal Asiatic Society*, Vol. 28, No. 3, p. 171.

Raffles' letter to Lord Minto of June 10, 1811, can be found in Chapter 3 of Lady Sophia Raffles, *Memoir of the Life and Public Services of Sir Thomas Stamford Raffles, with an introduction by John Bastin* (Singapore: Oxford University Press, 1991).

For definitions of "free trade empire" and "informal empire," see Bernard Porter, *The Lion's Share: A Short History of British Imperialism, 1850–1995* (London and New York: Longman, 1996), pp. 2–3; on conflict and cooperation between Britain and the Netherlands in the eighteenth and nineteenth centuries, see J.S. Bromley and E.H. Kossmann, eds., *Britain and the Netherlands in Europe and Asia: Papers delivered to the Third Anglo-Dutch Historical Conference* (London: Macmillan, 1968).

On the Bugis and Macassarese in Singapore, see C.M. Turnbull, *The Straits Settlements, 1826–67: Indian Presidency to Crown Colony* (Bristol: The Athlone Press, 1972), pp. 183–187; in Japanese, a good summary of the role of the Bugis can be found in Chapter 8, "Kaiiki sekai" [The Maritime World] of Tachimoto Narifumi, *Chiiki kenkyū no mondai to hōhō, shakai bunka seitai-rikigaku no kokoromi* [Problems and Methodologies in Regional Studies: An Attempt at a Study of the Dynamics of Social and Cultural Ecosystems], (Kyoto: Kyoto University Press, 1996).

On the history of nineteenth-century Singapore, see C.M. Turnbull, *The Straits Settlements, 1826–67*; on opium revenue farming, see Lee Poh Ping, *Chinese Society in Nineteenth Century Singapore* (Kuala Lumpur: Oxford University Press, East Asian Historical Monographs, 1978), and Carl A. Trocki, *Opium and Empire: Chinese Society in Colonial Singapore, 1800–1910* (Ithaca: Cornell University Press, 1990). On the "respectable Chinese," see my "Kamin goeisho no setsuritsu to kaitō" [The Establishment of the Chinese Protectorate and Secret Societies], in *Ajia kenkyū*, Vol. 22, No. 2 (1975), pp. 75–102. On the historical significance of revenue farming in nineteenth-century Southeast Asia, see John Butcher and Howard Dick, eds., *The Rise and Fall of Revenue Farming: Business Elites and the Emergence of the Modern State in Southeast Asia* (New York: St. Martin's Press, 1993).

Chapter Two: The Bugis Sea

On the tributary trade system, see Hamashita Takeshi, *Kindai Chūgoku no kokusai-teki keiki: Chōkō bōeki shisutemu to kindai Ajia* [The International Momentum of Modern China: The Tributary Trade System and Modern Asia], (Tokyo: University of Tokyo Press, 1990), and Hamashita Takeshi, "The Intra-Regional System in East Asia in Modern Times," in Peter J. Katzenstein and Shiraishi Takashi, eds., *Network Power: Japan and Asia* (Ithaca: Cornell University Press, 1997), pp. 113–135.

Raffles' 1808 report is included in C.E. Wurtzburg, *Raffles of the Eastern Isles*, pp. 68–81.

On the activities of the Bugis in the seventeenth and eighteenth centuries, see Dianne Lewis, *Jan Compagnie in the Straits of Malacca, 1641–1795* (Athens: Ohio University Press, 1995); M.C. Ricklefs, *A History of Modern Indonesia since c. 1300* (Stanford: Stanford University Press, 2nd ed., 1993), pp. 61–105; and Edward L. Poelinggomang, "The Dutch Trade Policy and Its Impact on Makassar's Trade," in *Review of Indonesian and Malaysian Affairs, Special Issue: Island Southeast Asia and the World Economy*, Vol. 27 (1993), pp. 61–76. On the prevalence of piracy at the time of Penang's founding, see K.C. Tregonning, *The British in Malaya: The First Forty Years, 1786–1826* (Tucson: University of Arizona Press, 1965).

Anthony Reid's estimates on population figures are taken from Anthony Reid, *Southeast Asia in the Age of Commerce, 1450–1680: Vol. One: The Lands below the Winds* (New Haven: Yale University Press, 1988), p. 15. Even today, the unbroken landscape of water and forests has not entirely disappeared from Southeast Asia. For one such description, see Tsubouchi Yoshihiro, *Shōjinkō sekai no jinkō-shi, Tōnan Ajia no fūdo to shakai* [A Demographic History of a World of Small Populations: The Climate and Society of Southeast Asia], (Kyoto: Kyoto University Press, 1998), Part 1, "Genzai no shōjinkō sekai: Shōjinkō sekai kikō" [The Small-Population World Today: Travels through the Small-Population World].

On the mandala system, see Chapters 1 and 2 of Oliver W. Wolters, *History, Culture, and Region in Southeast Asian Perspectives* (Singapore: Institute of Southeast Asian Studies, 1982). In Wolters' argument, the mandala only has meaning as a political system, and units like *negara* and *mueung* are not regarded as complete in themselves. In this sense, Wolters' ideas differ decisively from those of Clifford Geertz, who treats the *negara* as a self-contained system. It is often argued that Geertz's idea of the *negara* is a fantasy that ignores the "international" political and economic structure of nineteenth-century Southeast Asia; methodologically, because he treated the *negara* as a complete unit. See Clifford Geertz, *Negara: The Theatre State in Nineteenth-Century Bali* (Princeton, NJ: Princeton University Press, 1981).

On the destruction of the historical rhythm of the mandala world owing to the forces brought to bear by the Portuguese and the VOC, respectively, see Anthony Reid, *Southeast Asia in the Age of Commerce, 1450–1860, Vol. 2: Expansion and Crisis* (New Haven and London: Yale University Press, 1993), and M.C. Ricklefs, *A History of Modern Indonesia since c. 1300.*

CHAPTER THREE: TODDLING LEVIATHANS

This chapter is a revised and rewritten version of material previously published as Shiraishi Takashi, "Tōnan Ajia kokka-ron shiron" [An Essay at a Theory of States in Southeast Asia], in Tsubouchi Yoshihiro, ed., "*Sōgōteki chiiki kenkyū" o motomete, Tōnan Ajia-zō o tegakari ni* [In Search of Comprehensive Regional Studies, Guided by Images of Southeast Asia], (Kyoto: Kyoto University Press, 1999), pp. 261–281.

For Weber's definition of the state, see Max Weber, *Science as a Vocation*. U Nu's analogy is taken from U Nu, *U Nu: Saturday's Son* (New Haven: Yale University Press, 1975), pp. 135–136. Rajaratnam's remarks are taken from James Minchin, *No Man Is an Island: A Study of Singapore's Lee Kuan Yew* (Sydney, London, and Boston: Allen & Unwin, 1986). On the idea of the "nation," see Benedict Anderson, *Imagined Communities*, and the definition of the state in Benedict Anderson, "Old State, New Society: Indonesia's New Order in Comparative Historical Perspective," in *Language and Power: Exploring Political Cultures in Indonesia* (Ithaca: Cornell University Press, 1991), p. 95.

A pioneering study on the early development of leviathan states is J.S. Furnivall, *The Fashioning of Leviathan: The Beginnings of British Rule in Burma* (Rangoon: Burma Research Society, 1939). This is a classic early study on how the modern state was transplanted into Southeast Asia.

For the classic Javanese comparison of a king to a tiger, and his people to the forest, see Soemarsaid Moertono, *State and Statecraft in Old Java: A Study of the Later Mataram Period, 16th to 19th Century* (Ithaca: Southeast Asia Program, 1968), p. 22.

On the early history of Singapore, see C.M. Turnbull, *The Straits Settlements, 1826–67*; Lee Poh Ping, *Chinese Society in Nineteenth Century Singapore*; Carl A. Trocki, *Opium and Empire*; and C.M. Turnbull, *A History of Singapore, 1819–1988* (Singapore: Oxford University Press, 1989). On Java, see J.S. Furnivall, *Netherlands India: A Study of Plural Economy* (introduction by A.C.D. de Graeff, Cambridge University Press, 1939; reprinted 1967); Onghokham, "The Inscrutable and the Paranoid: An Investigation into the Sources of the Brotoningrat Affair," in Ruth T. McVey, ed., *Southeast Asian Transitions: Approaches through Social History* (New Haven: Yale Southeast Asia Studies, Yale University Press, 1978), pp. 112–157; and James Rush, *Opium to Java: Revenue Farming and Chinese Enterprise in Colonial Indonesia, 1860–1910* (Ithaca: Cornell University Press, 1990). On the Philippines, see Ikehata Setsuho and Ikuta Shigeru, *Sekai gendaishi 6: Tōnan Ajia gendaishi II: Firipin, Marēshia, Shingapōru* [Modern History of the World 6, Southeast Asia II: Philippines, Malaysia, Singapore], (Tokyo: Yamakawa Shuppansha Ltd., 1977), and Edgar Wickberg, *The Chinese in Philippine Life, 1850–1898* (New Haven and London: Yale University Press, 1965). Carl A. Trocki, *Opium and Empire*, and James Rush, *Opium to Java*, are the definitive studies on opium revenue farming in the Straits Settlements and Java during the nineteenth century. The remark by John Crawfurd about "one Chinaman equal in value . . ." is from Carl A. Trocki, *Opium, Empire and the Global Political Economy: A Study of the Asian Opium Trade, 1750-1950* (Abingdon-on-Thames: Routledge, 2012), p. 142.

CHAPTER FOUR: THE FORMATION OF PLURAL SOCIETIES

The quotation from Raffles is taken from Lady Sophia Raffles, *Memoir of the Life and Public Services of Sir Thomas Stamford Raffles*. The quotations from Lord Minto's letter to Lady Sophia are taken from C.E. Wurtzburg, *Raffles of the Eastern Isles*, pp.179–180. On the mestizo elite of Batavia and the social world during VOC rule, see Jean Gelman Taylor, *The Social World of Batavia: European and Eurasian in Dutch Asia* (Madison: University of Wisconsin Press, 1983).

Citations from *Hikayat Abdullah* [Life of Abdullah] and Thomson's description of Abdullah are taken from "The Hikayat Abdullah," trans. by A.H. Hill, *Journal of the Malayan Branch of the Royal Asiatic Society*, Vol. 28, No. 3.

Raffles' town plan is based on Maya Jayapal, *Old Singapore* (Kuala Lumpur: Oxford University Press, 1992), p. 1. My interpretation of the plan draws on C.M. Turnbull, *A History of Singapore, 1819–1988*.

My remarks on the politics of identity are a rewritten version of Shiraishi Takashi, "Saigo no nami no ato ni, 20-seiki nashonarizumu no sara naru bōken" [After the Last Wave: Further Adventures in Twentieth-Century Nationalism], in *Iwanami kōza gendai shakaigaku 24: Minzoku, kokka, esunishitī* [Iwanami Seminars on Modern Social Studies 24: Nation, State, Ethnicity], (Tokyo: Iwanami Shoten, Publishers, 1996), pp. 211–229. For a definition of the plural society, see J.S. Furnivall, *Colonial Policy and Practice: A Comparative Study of Burma and Netherlands India* (Cambridge: Cambridge University Press, 1948).

CHAPTER FIVE: THE LOGIC OF THE CIVILIZING PROJECT

This chapter is a revised and rewritten version of material that previously appeared in Japanese as "Indoneshia no kindai ni okeru watashi: Kartini no *ik* to Suwarudi no *saya*," [The "I" in Modern Indonesia: Kartini's *ik* and Soewardi's *saya*], *Tōnan Ajia kenkyū*, Vol. 34, No. 1 (June 1996), pp. 5–20.

Quotations from Couperus are from the English translation: Louis Couperus, *The Hidden Force*, trans. by Alexander Teizeira de Mattos (Amherst: University of Massachusetts Press, 1985).

The two maps are based on David Joel Steinberg, ed., *In Search of Southeast Asia: A Modern History*, revised edition (Honolulu: University of Hawaii Press, 1988). This volume (pp. 173–244) also contains a good summary of the political, economic, and social changes that took place in Southeast Asia at the end of the nineteenth and the beginning of the twentieth centuries. On the changes that took place in leviathan states in this period, see Thongchai Winichakul, *Siam Mapped: A History of the Geo-Body of a Nation* (Honolulu: University of Hawaii Press, 1997), and Shiraishi Takashi, "Anti-Sinicism in Java's New Order," in Daniel Chirot and Anthony Reid, eds., *Essential Outsiders: Chinese and Jews in the Modern Transformation of Southeast Asia and Central Europe* (Seattle and London: University of Washington Press, 1997), pp. 187–207.

For Kartini, I have drawn extensively on Tsuchiya Kenji, *Karutini no fūkei* [Kartini's Image of Java's Landscape], (Tokyo: Mekong, 1991). The quotation in English derives from Raden Adjeng Kartini, *Letters of a Javanese Princess*, translated from the Dutch by Agnes Louise Symmers (London: Duckworth & Co., 1921).

For the beginning of modern politics in the Dutch East Indies, see Shiraishi Takashi, *An Age in Motion: Popular Radicalism in Java, 1912–1926* (Ithaca: Cornell University Press, 1990), in which I also discuss Soewardi Soerjaningrat and his "Als ik eens Nederlander was," pp. 62–64.

For one example of a cultural crisis brought on by the transplantation and growth of leviathan into Southeast Asia, see Shiraishi Takashi, "Dangir's Testimony: Saminism Reconsidered," *Indonesia*, No. 50 (October 1990). On the formation of a prison camp archipelago and the idea of "No Trespass" signs, see Shiraishi Takashi, "The Phantom World of Digoel," *Indonesia*, No. 61 (April 1996), pp. 93–118, and "Policing the Phantom Underground," *Indonesia*, No. 63 (April 1997), pp. 1–46.

I drew on Furuya Jun for much of what I have to say on Americanism: Furuya Jun, "Amerikanizumu, sono rekishi-teki kigen to tenkai" [Americanism: Its Origins and Development], in Tōkyō daigaku shakai kagaku kenkyūjo, *20-seiki shisutemu (1) kōsō to keisei* [Twentieth-Century Systems 1: Structure and Formation], (Tokyo: University of Tokyo Press, 1998).

The statement attributed to Henry Ford is taken from Jonathan Schwartz, "Henry Ford's Melting Pot," in Otto Feinstein, ed., *Ethnic Groups in the City: Culture, Institutions, and Power*, Vol. 7 (Lexington, MA: Heath Lexington Books, 1971).

CHAPTER SIX: THE NEW IMPERIAL ORDER

This chapter is a rewritten version of Shiraishi Takashi, "Japan and Southeast Asia," and Peter J. Katzenstein and Shiraishi Takashi, "Conclusion: Region in World Politics, Japan and Asia—Germany in Europe," both in Peter J. Katzenstein and Shiraishi Takashi, eds., *Network Power: Japan and Asia*.

On George Kennan and the hand placed on Japan's jugular, see Bruce Cumings, "The Origins and Development of the Northeast Asian Political Economy: Industrial Sectors, Product Cycles and Political Consequences," in Frederic C. Deyo, ed., *The Political Economy of the New Asian Industrialism* (Ithaca: Cornell University Press, 1987), p. 61.

On the politics of productivity, see Charles S. Maier, "The Politics of Productivity: Foundations of American International Economic Policy after World War II," in Peter J. Katzenstein, ed., *Between Power and Plenty: Foreign Economic Policies of Advanced Industrial States* (Madison: University of Wisconsin Press, 1977), p. 23.

The quotation from Kishi Nobusuke is taken from Suehiro Akira, "The Road to Economic Re-Entry: Japan's Policy toward Southeast Asian Development in the 1950s and 1960s," in *Social Science Japan Journal*, Vol. 2, No. 1 (1999), pp. 85–105.

For James Fallows' view of Japanese economic activities in Southeast Asia as a type of Greater East Asian Co-Prosperity Sphere Mark II, see James Fallows, *Looking at the Sun: The Rise of the New East Asian Economic and Political System* (New York: Pantheon, 1994). On American hegemony in East Asia, see Bruce Cumings, "Japan and Northeast Asia into the Twenty-First Century," in Peter J. Katzenstein and Shiraishi Takashi, eds., *Network Power: Japan and Asia*.

On development systems, see Suehiro Akira, "Joshō: Kaihatsu-shugi to wa nani ka" [Preface: What Is Developmentalism?] and "1-shō hatten-tojō-koku no kaihatsu-shugi" [Part One: Developmentalism in Developing Countries], in Tokyo daigaku shakai kagaku kenkyūjo, *20-seiki shisutemu (4), kaihatsu-shugi* [Twentieth-Century Systems 4: Developmentalism], (Tokyo: University of Tokyo Press, 1998).

On the Americanization project, see Shiraishi Takashi, "Amerika wa naze tsuyoi no ka, hegemonī to chiteki kyōryoku" [Why Is the United States Strong: Hegemony and Intellectual Cooperation], *Chūō Kōron*, Vol. 113, No. 8 (July 1998), pp. 24–33.

Chapter Seven: Nation-State Building From Above

This chapter is largely reworked from material that previously appeared as Shiraishi Takashi, "Ue kara no kokka kensetsu: Tai, Indoneshia, Firipin" [Top-Down State-Building: Thailand, Indonesia, the Philippines], in *Kokusai Seiji*, No. 84 (February 1987), pp. 25–43, and "Ajia-gata seiji keizai taisei no owari to tsūka kiki" [The End of Asian-Model Political and Economic Systems and the Financial Crisis], in *Sekai* (May 1998), pp. 44–53.

On Thailand, see also Suehiro Akira, *Tai, kaihatsu to minshu-shugi* [Thailand: Development and Democracy], (Tokyo: Iwanami Shoten, Publishers, 1993), and Pasuk Phongpaichit and Chris Baker, *Thailand's Boom and Bust* (Chiang Mai: Silkworm Books, 1998); on Indonesia, see Shiraishi Takashi, *Shinpan Indoneshia* [Indonesia: New Edition], (Tokyo: NTT Publishing Co., Ltd., 1996); *Sukaruno to Suharuto* [Sukarno and Suharto], (Iwanami Shoten, Publishers, 1997); and *Hōkai* [Collapse], (Tokyo: NTT Publishing Co., Ltd., 1999).

On the concentration and expansion of power, see Samuel P. Huntington, *Political Order in Changing Societies* (New Haven: Yale University Press, 1968). On Marcos and the "revolution from the center," see Ferdinand E. Marcos, *Today's Revolution: Democracy* (Manila: Ferdinand E. Marcos, 1971). On the significance of the Aquino assassination, see Reynaldo C. Ileto, "The Past in the Present Crisis," in R.J. May and Francisco Nemenzo, eds., *The Philippines after Marcos* (London: Croom Helm, 1984).

Chapter Eight: Thinking About Asia

Part of this chapter appeared in a different form in Peter J. Katzenstein and Shiraishi Takashi, "Conclusion: Region in World Politics, Japan and Asia-Germany in Europe," in Peter J. Katzenstein and Shiraishi Takashi, eds., *Network Power: Japan and Asia*.

On the global significance of Asian industrialization, see Hara Yōnosuke, "Kiseki kara kiki e, soshite sono go" [From Miracle to Crisis, and Beyond], in Hara Yōnosuke, ed., *Ajia keizai-ron* [Essays on Asian Economies], (NTT Publishing Co., Ltd., 1999), and Sugihara Kaoru, *Ajia Taiheiyō-ken no kōryū* [The Rise and Fall of the Asia-Pacific Region], (Osaka: Osaka University Press, 2003).

For the definition of maritime Asia, see Hamashita Takeshi, "Jo: Chiiki kenkyū to Ajia" [Preface: Regional Studies and Asia], in *Ajia kara kangaeru 2: Chiiki shisutemu*, [Thinking from Asia 2: Regional Systems], (Tokyo: University of Tokyo Press, 1993).

On the history of China, I drew on Ichiko Chūzō, *Sekai no rekishi 20: Chūgoku no kindai* [History of the World 20: Modern China], (Tokyo: Kawade Shobo Shinsha, Publishers, 1990).

For the section on Japan, see Nakamura Takafusa, *Shōwa-shi I: 1926–1945* [History of the Showa Era Part I: 1926–1945], (Tokyo: Toyo Keizai Inc., 1993).

INDEX

(pic) refers to a photo, illustration, or map page.

Bowring Treaty 122–23
Britain 15, 35 (pic)
British empire 90 (pic)
  colonies/posts 17–18, 20, 22–23, 33, 59, 108, 141, 143, 145
  formal 25, 58, 145
  free trade 25–36, 48, 50, 52–60, 64, 66, 105, 122–23, 132, 140, 154
  informal 10, 19 (pic), 25, 34, 50, 56, 58, 145
  new 11, 24–25, 32, 36, 39, 42, 44, 59, 71, 145
British Malaya See Malaya (Malaysia)
British ships 27 (pic), 50
Brooke, J. 57 (pic)
Bugis (Buginese) 20, 25–26, 32, 36–42, 48, 56–58, 79–81, 80 (pic)
Bugis adventurers 40, 48, 56–58
Bugis century 39–42
"Bugis season" 26
Bugis-Macassarese 20, 25–26, 39–40
buildings, Malacca 14, 36–37
bureaucratic state 122–24, 127–29, 132, 135–36
Burma (Myanmar) 19 (pic), 35 (pic), 42, 44 (pic), 45, 51, 90 (pic), 97, 115, 120–21, 144, 160, 167

C

Calcutta 15, 16, 24
Cambodia 19 (pic), 40, 90 (pic), 112, 167
camphor 38, 39
Canada 141
Cantonese 56, 79, 91
Cape of Good Hope 15, 24
capitalism 10, 57–58, 89, 92, 100, 116–17, 140, 144, 146, 150, 154–55
cash crops 29, 60–61, 64
Catholic church 65, 136
Cebu 66, 144
Celebes (Sulawesi) 14, 16, 17, 19 (pic), 20, 24–26, 32, 37–42, 44 (pic), 81
censuses 81–82, 91

centers vs borders 43–46, 52–53, 88, 90 (pic), 145, 153
  See also revolution from the center; Sinocentrism
Ceylon 15, 24
Chakri dynasty 50, 59, 82, 122–23, 127, 145
Chao Phraya River 19 (pic), 123
China 10, 14, 19 (pic), 21, 24–26, 45–47, 54–55, 64, 106, 108–9, 111, 113, 123, 140, 141, 144, 145–55, 159, 162–68. See also People's Republic of China; Sinocentrism
"China Dream" 165
Chinese immigration 55–56, 58, 61, 66–67, 81, 92, 123, 145
Chinese languages 56, 79, 91
Chinese nationalism 149, 165
Chinese networks 29–30, 32–37, 39, 40, 45, 46–48, 50, 55–56, 61–63, 91–92, 145, 153, 154, 161
  See also overseas Chinese
Chinese peoples 28, 55, 63 (pic)
  relationship with British 21, 23–26, 32–36, 92
  relationship with Dutch 21, 23, 82, 87–88
  ethnicity 21, 65, 70, 71, 77, 78–81, 83, 86–87, 89
  in Java 21, 22, 38, 60, 61–62, 65, 82, 86–88, 91–92
  in Malacca 28, 29, 37, 77, 78, 82
  in Malaya 18, 26, 28, 56–58, 81, 82–83
  in the Philippines 65–67, 82, 132
  in Singapore 24–26, 28–29, 32–33, 35–36, 54–55, 56–57, 79–81, 80 (pic), 89, 145
  in Southeast Asia 24, 26, 29, 33–35, 45–46, 48, 54, 81, 83, 89, 91, 92, 145, 152–54
  in Straits Settlements 29, 30, 53–58, 61–62, 81, 91, 92, 145
  See also coolie labor; overseas Chinese; private trade; "respectable Chinese"; secret societies, Chinese; tributary trade

About the Author

Born in 1950 in Ehime, Japan, Shiraishi Takashi majored in international relations at the University of Tokyo in 1972 and obtained his Ph.D. in History from Cornell University in 1986. Shiraishi has lectured at the University of Tokyo (1979–87), Cornell University (1987–98), Kyoto University (1996–2005), and the National Graduate Institute for Policy Studies (GRIPS) in Tokyo (2005–09). He has served as an executive member of the Council for Science and Technology Policy (CSTP) of the Cabinet Office of the Government of Japan (2009–12), president of GRIPS (2011–17), president of the Institute of Developing Economies-Japan External Trade Organization (2007–18), and professor of international relations, Ritsumeikan University (2017–18). As of this writing, he serves as chancellor of the Prefectural University of Kumamoto, a post he has held since 2018.

Shiraishi has additionally served as editor of *Indonesia*, a publication of the Cornell Southeast Asia Program (1986–2000), and editor in chief of nippon.com (2011–14), a multilingual online journal. In 2007, he was awarded the Medal of Honor with Purple Ribbon, a civilian honor which is given by the Government of Japan in recognition of distinct accomplishment in academia and the arts. In 2016, he was also named a Japanese Person of Cultural Merit. In 2017, he received the Honorary Medal of Bintang Jasa Utama from the Republic of Indonesia for his contributions to Indonesian development in economic and educational affairs.

Shiraishi has published many books, three of which have won awards: *An Age in Motion* (Ithaca: Cornell University Press, 1990), which received the Ohira Masayoshi Asia Pacific Award; *Indoneshia: Kokka to seiji* [Government and Politics in Indonesia], (Tokyo: Libroport Co., 1992), a winner of the Suntory Prize for Social Sciences and Humanities; and the Japanese edition of the present volume, *Umi no teikoku* (Tokyo: CHUOKORON-SHINSHA INC., 2000), a recipient of the Yomiuri Yoshino Sakuzo Prize. His other works include *Chūgoku wa Higashi-Ajia o dou kaeruka* [How Is China Changing East Asia?], (co-authored with Caroline Sy Hau, Tokyo: CHUO-KORON-SHINSHA INC., 2012); *Kaiyō Ajia vs. tairiku Ajia*, translated as *Maritime Asia vs. Continental Asia* by Lynne Rienner Publishers (Kyoto: Minerva Shobo, 2016); and *Emerging States and Economies: Their Origins, Drivers, and Challenges Ahead* (co-edited with Sonobe Tetsushi, Singapore: Springer, 2019).

（英文版）海の帝国　アジアをどう考えるか
Empire of the Seas: Thinking about Asia

2021年3月27日　第1刷発行

著　者　　　白石　隆
英　訳　　　公益財団法人日本国際問題研究所
発行所　　　一般財団法人出版文化産業振興財団
　　　　　　〒101-0051 東京都千代田区神田神保町2-2-30
　　　　　　電話　03-5211-7283
　　　　　　ホームページ　https://www.jpic.or.jp/

印刷・製本所　　大日本印刷株式会社